A Normal Life

(Rants and Reflections)

By

Jim McGarrah

ISBN: 978-93-6354-092-7

First Edition: 2025
Rs. 200/-

Cyberwit.net
HIG 45 Kaushambi Kunj, Kalindipuram
Allahabad - 211011 (U.P.) India
http://www.cyberwit.net
Tel: +(91) 9415091004
E-mail: info@cyberwit.net

Printed at Repro India Limited.

Acknowledgements

Thanks to Ink Brush Press, Traces Magazine, Indiana Historical Society Press, and the Princeton Clarion, for publishing some of this content along with Rochak Publishing. Thanks to Robin Wright, editor supreme, and my daughter, Leslie for producing the cover art.

I dedicate this book to the memory of my uncle, Jim Huffman, who was a kind man overburdened by life and his memories of combat in World War II.

Contents

Just the Way Things Were

Long before computers compiled the line from Vegas or satellites carried major sports on closed circuit TV, we had the Palace Pool Room. On the weekends, my old man sat me by a radio that housed flowing tubes of light. Those tubes produced sound from their brightness, a sort of Motorola synesthesia. Magically, the screeching, hissing, static would sometimes form actual words – Hodges…swings…back…against… wall. It's gone…Dodgers…two runs…two hits…no errors – as I leaned into the noise to concentrate. More wondrous than the talking box was the ticker tape machine that rose next to it from a rickety table with uneven legs. It seemed a simple enough device, a few small gears and a tiny roll of paper on a metal spindle beneath a glass dome. Yet, at the end of each inning of every major league baseball game being played on any day during the summer, the gears rattled and hummed, turning paper through an ink-fed punch. The clacking sound reminded me of Southern Freight trains pounding over loose tracks at the Hall Street crossing by Lowell Elementary School.

As the ribbon of paper tracked through a slight opening near the bottom of the glass globe, someone sitting nearby tore it off, stretched it out arm's length, and read off the ball scores from around the country that had been etched into the white surface with black ink. Over the clang and thump of nearby pinball machines, whoever confiscated the enchanted strip screamed out the numbers and the names – "Cardinals 4, Dodgers 6, 5th inning." "Yankees 2, Red Sox Nothing, 8th inning"— like a sideshow barker at the county fair. Depending on who had money placed where, these reports were often followed by words my father never allowed me to say, especially around my mother.

One more sound always completed the cycle every fifteen or twenty minutes. A small man with a shaved head and a toothless grin scratched the information across a screeching chalkboard. His name was George and he had been orphaned as a young child. George fit the description of what we now call a developmentally disabled person. Back then, people had less sensitive language to use. We labeled him our local retarded guy because he could barely read and seemed happy working for tips.

George wasn't always treated with kindness by the clientele, me included as I grew into a teenager. But he also wasn't nearly as dumb as we believed. A couple of older kids had given George a lit cherry bomb when he was very small and called it candy. The firecracker exploded in his mouth and his face took on a sad, twisted, grimace afterwards that was enhanced by his lack of teeth and his slovenly speech patterns. Big Jim, who owned the pool room, helped George save his tip money in the bank and rented him a room at the Emerson Hotel. Because of Jim's generosity and guidance, George managed to save a good sum of money and live a comfortable life for many years. As time went by, the man became an icon and probably more recognizable in the tri-state area than the town mayor. Even George's eventual downfall remains the stuff of legend. Unknown to Big Jim, he withdrew his savings, took a bus to St. Louis and hired a hooker for a night. The adventure ruined George in many ways, and he ended up in the county home for indigents. That's a story for another time.

Baseball was hardly the only thing you could bet on. In those Eisenhower days after WWII, the white men folk of rural Southern Indiana felt confident and prosperous enough to bet on anything. Most of them had been through the horrific experience of a war, and, as odd as it may seem, gambling replaced that need for an adrenalin rush with far less risk. One day, I must have been ten years old, Mr. Land, a notorious liar who stuttered when he lied, sat on a bench by the ticker tape machine. He said, "It is so hot today that I'll bbbbbe dddddamned if I dddidn't fry eggs and bbacon on the sidewalk in front of my house this mmmmorning, just to save a little on my utttility bbill."

The Cardinals were losing and Mr. Archer, who always bet on them, spit a stream of tobacco toward the brass spittoon with a sigh.

"You're a fucking liar," said Doodlebug Rainey while playing a game of snooker.

"I c…c…can prove it"

"I got ten bucks says you can't."

By now, the entire room had gone quiet. A challenge had been offered and money was on the line. Some men reached into their pockets wanting to sweeten the pot, but mostly no one was willing to bet against Doodlebug, who won his wagers frequently. Through the blue cigar smoke, above the hum of the ceiling fan, over an occasional nervous cough, and beyond the scent of cooking onions, the voice of authority boomed. "I'll back Doodlebug but only 3 to 2." Big Jim, the owner of the establishment, had offered to book all bets on Doodlebug but at the payoff rate of one dollar for every two dollars someone wagered. It seemed like a good investment to most of the guys. As matter of fact, it seemed like a sure thing. Concrete was porous and could never heat up enough to fry an egg.

On the other hand, Big Jim was not a gambler. He made book and that was business. Jim never did anything stupid. If he thought Mr. Land had no shot at winning, he would never have taken any money at all. The gambling fever rose to a frenzy, and some of the old boys figured Jim knew some egg-frying science that they weren't aware of and planned to cash in on his secret knowledge. Money started coming in on both sides now, which had been the plan all along. With enough money bet both ways, Jim could pay off either side, keep his house cut of 20%, and end up making a clear profit no matter what happened.

When the furor subsided, the short order cook behind the counter handed Land an unbroken egg. Doodlebug said, "Prove your point, or not" and out the door they went, followed by the entire crowd, about ten men in all. Women weren't allowed in the pool rooms in those days before Gloria Steinem and Cosmopolitan magazine. The crowd on the sidewalk drew the attention of others around the town square. I saw clerks from the courthouse across the street crowd against the windows, their curiosity overwhelming their work ethic. Shoppers strolled out of the Ben Franklin Five & Dime store and peered at the large circle of sweating men. Greek's Candy Store emptied its tables and soda fountain stools as the loafers in there followed the commotion.

Land stepped ceremoniously to the center, kneeled, and cracked the egg on the curb. Splitting the shell apart slowly, he let the egg white drip out onto the hot concrete until the yolk squeezed out whole and plopped in the center of the puddle. At first nothing happened. The circle tightened and everyone leaned in. Someone threw an elbow into Bill Wheeler's ribs, jostling for a better position. Doodlebug got down on his hands and knees next to the egg. With his face almost flush on the sidewalk, he stared at the edges of the egg puddle. I did too, and I swear the borders of that egg began turning white like you might see one do in a skillet that was just heating up. But before it could be called one way or the other, one of Roy Swain's mangy old dogs crept into the circle as if it was a henhouse and sucked that egg, yolk and all, down his gullet and then licked the sidewalk clean. Roy, who had no interest in the doings of other humans, whistled and the dog rejoined the pack, which disappeared around the corner. A collective groan and cries of "foul" "unfair" "redo" echoed around the circle.

Everyone who reads this and lived in my small town at the time will remember that story differently, especially if that reader happens to be male and hung around the pool room in the late nineteen-fifties. It quickly became legend, and every legend has many versions. This, however, is my story. If you think of the scene as happening some other way, write your own story. The point is simple; gambling thrived as an illegal form of entertainment even though frowned upon by the righteous. It provided a necessary form of release from the monotony of life in those days. What got frowned on in public often got accepted with quiet acquiescence in private, like drinking during the Prohibition Era. That's just the way things were, and the Palace held an honored place as the center of that nefarious enterprise in all of Gibson County.

The county elected a new prosecuting attorney every few years. The lawyers always swore by all that was holy to stamp out bookmaking and pinball playing at the Palace. They made these blood oaths like Eliot Ness at every church ice cream social, PTA meeting, and Rotary Club breakfast for weeks before the elections. The week after the election, the pool room regulars could count on a dramatic raid. This became sacrosanct for a newly elected prosecutor after Robert Stack came on TV starring in the *Untouchables*. We were never disappointed. Ironically, once the Daily Clarion newspaper carried the front-page story of the raid complete with pictures, the prosecutors always found themselves back in the pool room a week or so later to eat an egg sandwich and check the morning line on the Cardinals game. It was just the way things were. If you've been paying attention to Congress lately, you'll realize that most people never question the ethics of behavior that is attached to the movement of money, especially if they stand a chance of getting some.

That brings me to the actual thought process that started this little journey down Nostalgia Lane, a visit to my old hometown and a drive around. Much family-owned business in the town center has slowly evaporated, carried away on the winds of corporate America. Some shops have been replaced with other enterprises. The Palace is still there as a diner but without pool tables and pinball machines and without the characters who gave my little town a soul. A few new businesses struggle to stay open and refurbish the small-town ambience that made the fifties and sixties a special time for me as I grew up. The problem with this commendable attempt lies more with end result than effort. Attitudes about nutrition, taste, and atmosphere have changed dramatically over the decades, and those changes violate the true authenticity of the old places.

The Farmer's Daughter serves excellent food and deserves all the support it can get. The menu shines but with hipster fare that is actually healthy to eat. Turkey and peach chutney with sharp cheddar on brioche, ham and cheddar quiche, pasta salad with fresh spinach and fresh mozzarella, roasted peppers and balsamic vinegar, Ribollita soup, and for dessert, white chocolate truffles among other tasty delights are all available. On the other hand, coney dogs, chili with spaghetti, fried eggs and bacon with biscuits and sausage gravy, Twinkies, Snowballs, and French fries cooked in beef tallow, all the mainstays of a young boy's Eisenhower era diet, are not.

A karaoke bar replaces Art Miller's Tavern. In the old days, my father and his friends sang along with a Wurlitzer jukebox to Patsy Cline and Johnny Cash as they rolled dice across the bar for drinks. They bitched about an income tax rate well over 50%, argued over who might win the pennant, discussed the crazy notion that a Catholic might become president, and worried whether or not they could afford an extra hundred dollars a month to put their kids through college. The idea that a narcissist could get on stage and pretend to be a famous singer because his or her own life was too miserable to live would never have gained any traction with a generation that had just returned from World War II. You can still get beer on tap at the bar, but most of it is "light" or micro-brewed, "girly" beers as my father called them.

On the northeast corner, the empty shell of the former J.C. Penny's store oversees the ghosts of Rogers Army & Navy Surplus and Hudson Furniture. Index Notions is now a bland Chinese buffet, and the Citizens Bank building has collapsed into a memorial rock garden. Shelby Stevens Clothing, The Model, Heldt's Shoes, the places where my mother always bought me new stuff to wear for Easter church service have morphed into nick-nack shops, antique stores—a metaphor for junk that didn't sell at the last yard sale—and a couple of sparsely populated professional offices. As I write these words, Greeks Candy Store and Soda Fountain, the most popular after school hangout for three generations, is being boarded up to make the area more presentable for non-existent investors and tourists.

This downtown desertion began, as urban sprawl always does, with the development of the outer west side limits of town. First came K-Mart, followed by McDonald's, KFC, Burger King, Big Lots, Show Shoe, and most importantly Wal-Mart. The local banks merged with larger regional banks that later merged with larger national banks that built new branches by Wal-Mart and across the street from McDonald's.

The "progress" I'm describing isn't unique to Princeton, Indiana. It has happened over the last forty years in myriad towns and villages all over the country and hasn't always been a bad thing. Job possibilities increase and even though these jobs are often unskilled and underpaid, it's still employment. Options for purchasing goods and services rise exponentially, along with opportunities for food and entertainment. Hell, Princeton recently opened an Applebee's and an automatic car wash. Gambling is legal now.

Besides that, we all tend to overromanticize the past. While I was busy living an idyllic small town WASP life, blacks were being turned away from the Palace, forced to sit in the balcony at the movie theater, drink from separate water fountains and until reaching junior high, attend segregated schools. Women could not borrow money for a successful business venture without a male co-signer, were relegated mostly to menial tasks around the home, could not divorce their abusive husbands without being ostracized in the community, and earned half of what their male counterparts did even if they managed to luck into the same type work.

Still, there remains an inherent sadness in me when I think of the simple pleasures abandoned by this new paradigm of society. Things will never be just the way they were in 1960, and while that means the quality of our lives has improved in many ways, it also means that we've lost some of the qualities and some of the values that gave Americans everywhere a sense of community, a collective compassion for neighbors, and bonds of friendship that in many ways superseded blood relation. Is it possible to make progress by not moving forward, by restricting ourselves to the past? The answer is no. There are negatives and positives in every era. Human nature dictates that, as we grow older, our memories become infused with imagination and our prospective on the past gets over romanticized. We remember the good and embellish it. Often, we forget to learn from the bad.

On the other hand, I think we make progress in the intrinsic values, beyond the temporal, that truly define us as human beings, only if we hold on to the pieces of the past that anchor those values such as kinship, compassion, responsibility to community, and self-sacrifice, in us. Then they become a springboard to understanding and bettering ourselves. A famous horseman, Monty Richards, once said, "A good trainer can hear a horse speak to him. A great trainer can hear a horse whisper." This is true of life as well. A good human can hear life speaking from the past and a great one can hear it whisper.

Jimmy Hayes and the Hunters

I wish I could remember the name of the lake. That's the thing about getting old. When you're young, a memory is more like a movie. Events and places and people, they all flow in a straightforward story as they occurred. Of course, like a film, actions and characters are often embellished with heroic perspective, especially if the person remembering is also the star. Regardless, they seem to progress in a chronological order creating a coherent narrative that satisfies the reason for the memory in the first place.

When you have lived for as long as I have, memories take on the appearance of old photographs, sometimes faded and cracked and as if they've been placed in an album in no particular order and pop up randomly from page to page. You are left to create form and substance for the whole series from the chaos of time. So, back to the point. I don't remember the name of the lake, only that it was summer and the year was probably 1971 or '72. The lake was a large open area bordered by trees on two sides, a highway on the third, and between the highway and the water a tangled line of bushes, weeds, and a few more scrawny trees. It was large enough that I can't describe the far shore at all. I'm sure one existed, but all I see now is a vanishing point like a Monet painting.

It was close to Chester, New York. That village was my home then. Chester had everything my burned-out, war-scarred, drug-addled mind and body required at the age of twenty-two. Supportive friends, beautiful young women, a working-class tavern with cheap drinks, music, and the Catskill Mountains. My memory got to this lake and Jimmy Hayes through the reflective path of the past. I stop occasionally in the memory of Chester as it was a happy time and the only time in my life when I've felt truly and completely in harmony with the two sides of human existence. The great poet, Mary Oliver, once labeled those two sides—leisure and labor. They are natural external forces that we humans reconcile internally. We need both. I am a restless soul who has never been very comfortable unless I'm performing a task. Simply enjoying life for being life has always been difficult for me. It felt comfortable to do that among these people at this time and place, a feeling that has remained ambiguous ever since I left there in 1973.

This day had proved that leisure was possible even for me. The sun flooded the lake with shimmering diamonds forged by light and water. Creatures slipped through the forest almost unnoticed. Squirrels, rabbits, quail, meadowlarks flitted across small open patches of ground beneath the trees around us. Colors were everywhere and bright. Yellows and deep greens, blues and purples from the twisting vines, ferns, moss, and mountain flowers on the forest floor exploded all around the perimeter of the lake. In all honesty, I think the vividness may have been enhanced by a bowl of hash my friend Jimmy Hayes and I smoked as we watched a carload of our female buddies spill out from said car and run across the beach into the water. Their tanned flesh and lithe athletic bodies splashed and shivered through our fantasies in images that would fill this 21st century politically correct era with an angst we never considered in this morally free one.

Several other people dotted the lake shore, and Jimmy and I rested joyfully on the beach, our backs nesting in the warm sand and our eyes glazed over reflecting clouds and blue sky. I was in the moment of serene sleep/not-sleep when Hayes bolted upright and spoke loudly.

"What the fuck?"

"What the fuck," I repeated.

"Do you see what I see?"

"I hope not you crazy bastard."

"Over there just inside the tree line."

He pointed to his left and there, about fifty yards from the shore in a tangle of brush and leering out across the water, were three guys that from a distance looked to be about our age. They wore camouflage shirts and pants and cradled either rifles or shotguns in their arms. It was a little too far away to be sure. They stood erect and motionless.

"Hunters?" I asked.

"Yeah, either hunters or characters from *Deliverance*."

We were both fans of James Dickey and had recently read his novel, a current bestseller about the sordid adventures of a camping party run afoul of backwoods hillbilly sodomites.

"Let's go. This ain't hunting season and they don't look like birdwatchers."

Jimmy was right. No one hunted in this area, not even during the autumn when it was legal. The lake existed too close to civilization. Even the amateurs looking to bag a deer, the doctors and lawyers, and stockbrokers from New York City who bought a license once a year and tramped around the woods during deer season in November putting local cows and horses in jeopardy, had enough common sense to refrain from the off-limit areas in the Catskills. The game wardens would not hesitate to confiscate their expensive equipment and level outrageous fines.

It might seem reckless for two unarmed and stoned hippies to approach armed strangers. Actually, it was reckless. But Jimmy Hayes and I had spent the last part of the 1960's in heavy combat. Vietnam remained very close to the surface of our minds in those days, and while we both relished being alive, we missed the adrenaline rush and euphoria experienced in a firefight as well. It took me years to get over the paradox of fear and excitement that occurred when placing myself in danger. Taking chances can be addictive. We jumped up and moved quickly toward the three strange young men. They, on the other hand, watched us with expressions of confusion and disbelief. The confrontation lasted only a couple of minutes.

"What do you think you're doing?" Jimmy Hayes asked the young man in front. The other two were a couple of steps behind on the right and left. A triangle of dumbness, I thought, and that dumbness made the situation risky.

"Why is that your business?" The one in front—a tall, thin fellow with short brown hair, a two-day stubble, and a crooked nose—spoke, baring his teeth in what an optimist would call a smile and I recall as a snarl.

"You have guns. It isn't hunting season and this area is off limits anyway," said Hayes.

"We got permission from the owner to bag us a few squirrels."

"What's the owner's name?"

As I asked the question, I noticed his weapon was a breech-loading single shot .410 shotgun, old and cheap, but deadly. Even stoned, I noted the hunter's knuckles whitened and tightened on the stock as well. I'll never know what action was running through his mind. Maybe he wanted to shoot us; maybe he was frustrated because of our presence and felt he had to turn around and leave. I'll never know because in the same instant, Jimmy Hayes, who was already close enough to the guy to kiss him, shot his left arm out, grabbed the gun, broke the breech open, and popped the shotgun shell out. It fell to the ground. The guy's two buddies seemed frozen. Their mouths open in disbelief, neither pointed their guns in our direction. The tall one in front looked shocked and took a step back but managed to squeal out a few words.

"Hey, that's my gun."

"And, you can have it back when you turn your ass around and move off," Jim said.

"Hey, why'd you grab it?"

"I didn't want you to blow your foot off," said Jimmy.

"Come on, man, gimme my gun back. We don't want any trouble."

"Will you leave?"

They all nodded, and Hayes handed him the empty .410. None of them spoke. They spun around and walked off through the trees.

"You could have gotten us killed."

"Nah, they weren't killers, just wannabe's."

Jimmy Hayes was right. He had a certain sense about people, and as far as I know, he never sized a situation up wrong for as long as I knew him, except one. Like all of us when we were young, he misjudged the meaning of mortality. He thought he was immortal.

The other two had made no hostile movements. They were just kids, really, shocked at his behavior and as scared and embarrassed as I was nervous. Hayes never blinked. The gun owner did. In retrospect, it seems like an old "High Noon" western standoff. But it was more like a "Blazing Saddles" comedy. These fellows were not killers, and never would be, but I didn't know it at the time. We had both seen stone-cold killers in the past. I had even been shot by one. Maybe Jimmy sensed what he said he sensed. Maybe he didn't care one way or another. So, you can think of Jimmy Hayes as a brave guy, which he probably was. Or you can think of him as reckless and a little stupid, which he probably was also. He could also be brash and annoying. But what made us such good friends is that I knew he would always do what he believed was right, even if it wasn't convenient or beneficial to him. That was a rare quality then, and it's even rarer today in a world full of people who seem to see courage, compassion, empathy, and integrity as weaknesses. They aren't. Those are the qualities that allow us to have a workable society.

I always felt that Jimmy Hayes would have made a good senator for the great state of New York, maybe on the order of a Ted Kennedy who was called "the lion of the Senate." But, the sensitivity required when humans exercise those good qualities I just mentioned can bring sadness with them as well. That's the other side of the coin because the truth is most people are more concerned with their own rewards rather than the self-sacrifice that is also required in an honest life. When a sensitive person understands this truth, that the dream of a grand conscience raising for all of humanity is an illusion and not realistic, it can lead to self-destructive behavior. I have learned this based on my experience with humans, both good and bad.

More than twenty years had passed since I last saw Jimmy. I was on my way to a writer's conference in Vermont. He lived in Massachusetts, so I made a little detour. And more than twenty-five years had passed since we raised our beer bottles together at the Chester Inn in a toast to the great hippie revolution that was supposed to usher in the Utopia of sex, drugs, and rock & roll that never happened. Jimmy spent those years in excess, too much alcohol, too many cigarettes, too many lovers, too little love, and a lot of lost hope. Yes, he had finally stabilized his life. He built a home with a good person, and she shared with him a child to raise. He quit smoking, left drugs behind, drank in moderation, and arrived at a peaceful place with his memories and his self. Our visit was joyful, and I drove to Vermont.

At the conference as I talked about line breaks, narratives, plots, imagery, and all the tools writers use in our search for voice, style, and vision, I got a phone call. Jimmy, a person who lived all three of those qualities, barely fifty years old, had died of a heart attack. In the grand scheme of things, I suppose his death was no more than a blip on some god's radar and a minor bump on the road most of us travel. But I don't see how his early departure from humanity made us better off. In these days when morons, buffoons, cowards, and self-serving assholes pass themselves off as corporate leaders, statesmen, preachers, and even some teachers, and when we seem bereft of ethics and honesty, I wish Jim Hayes was still around.

Synthesis

One of the most crucial intellectual concepts in our society, the ability to connect disparate thoughts in viable ways, must be learned and relearned and re-relearned until it becomes instinctive at all ages and levels of life. It cannot be inherited or produced through genetic manipulation or soaked in through some osmotic process. Synthesis thinking, the amalgamation of ideas, presents us with a means to rise above what author William Golding calls the third or lowest level of thinking, which is not thinking at all but rather, feeling.

His tertiary label stems from observing that most people in America today seem to accept answers that agree with their emotional bias, serve their personal interest best, and require the least amount of effort to research. In other words, whatever feels like the right answer must therefore be the right answer. This shallow approach to complex issues is devoid of critical analysis of the big picture. It eliminates possibilities and ignores my old man's favorite saying that "no matter how thin you slice bread, it always has two sides." He repeated this mantra to me frequently after losing an argument with my mother. Consequently, what is best for the most in our society is relegated often to the trash heap of ideas or never gets considered at all.

Through the method of synthesis, however, we can realize the answer to important questions such as why pay taxes, vote, work, shop, save, build, and live collectively under a democratic form of government that leaves itself open to individualism by its very nature. Synthesis operates this way. Idea A enters the mind through some external stimulus, rumbling around unchecked until idea B enters in a similar manner. It's only a matter of time before one bumps into the other. A courtship begins, followed by copulation. Idea C, the offspring of this often-unholy union, could not exist without A and B. But the idea matures rapidly as a separate entity. Maintaining knowledge from both A and B, C transcends their boundaries to become something totally different and greater than the sum of its parts when separated. It is a miracle equal to, if not surpassing, the Rally's Big Buford with cheese. Consider the following paradigm.

A man drives from Louisville to Lexington, 68 miles over partially paved Kentucky roads, for the express purpose of gambling. This man is a short, chubby, old guy called ME who could have spent his meager funds on more worthwhile endeavors, say an evening at the Irish Rover Pub, rather than trying to pick the one horse that might stick its neck in front of ten or twelve other horses crossing an invisible line after running around a circle of synthetic dirt called polytrack. On this day, though, an old friend of Mine (possessive of ME), was running a filly named Brilliant Autumn in the third race, and she had a good shot at winning and paying a decent price.

This was exactly what happened. The weather was miserable, gray, misting rain, blustery, and twenty degrees below normal for mid-April in Kentucky. But Brilliant Autumn made the sun shine in my heart, more importantly my pocketbook, by romping to a four-length win over a decent field and paying 12.40 for every 2.00 I bet. This experience felt much more rewarding than most of my experiences with human females over the years; however, the reason I brought it up has more to do with structure than content. The tale serves a simple purpose in the broader narrative. According to Wiki answers.com a trigger incident is what starts a story. I prefer Richard Hugo's definition in that a trigger incident is what starts a poem, but that's just my own idiosyncrasy. Sometimes you may retain the trigger, and sometimes it may be eliminated upon revision. In this case, it gets me from my home to Lexington in the first place, without which no synthesis of ideas would have occurred and provided me with a theory for the recent demise of democracy in our country along with a possible solution to the abundance of idiotic, corrupt, sexually deviant, and narcissistic fools infiltrating the Congress of the United States of America.

Being flush as they say in gambling parlance, I rented a room for the night in a place cheaper than Motel 6 and possibly owned by a Hichcockian-looking fellow named Bates. Then, I ate a celebratory meal in my room consisting of various delicacies from the KFC next to the motel. I retired after this epicurean delight for some reading rather than watching a rerun of the Bachelorette on TV. That's when it happened. The fusion of two small thoughts turned into a Jesus-level profundity of such consequence that, if adapted by our great unwashed masses, our 99%, America might once again become a free nation instead of ruled by the 1%.

For you, dear reader, to understand the implications created by my brain, I need to quote a passage from Hunter Thompson's *Kingdom of Fear*, the book I was reading in bed, and juxtapose it with a tourist brochure—more synthesis. It sounds trickier than it really is. This is what I read:

A Willingness to Argue, however violently, implies a faith of something basic in the antagonist, an assumption that he is still open to argument and reason and, if all else fails, then finely orchestrated persuasion in the form of political embarrassment. The 1960's were full of examples of good, powerful men changing their minds on heavy issues: John Kennedy on Cuba and the Bay of Pigs, Martin Luther King Jr. on Vietnam, Gene McCarthy on "working behind the scenes and within the Senate Club," Robert F. Kennedy on long hair and what eventually came to be Freak Power, Ted Kennedy on Francis X. Morrissey, and Senator Sam Ervin on wiretaps and preventative detention. Anyway, the general political drift of the 1960's was one of the Good Guys winning, slowly but surely (and even clumsily sometimes) over the Bad Guys.

As I read this, I realized that Thompson—a Moses type prophet for us Boomers—had been correct. In America, we have always believed that good eventually triumphs over evil, and we have always had men who acted in accordance with that principal, statesmen unafraid of rethinking their attitudes if the result of the adjustment produced a better result for society. After all, representing the majority interests is what politicians were elected to do. Unfortunately, something has changed in the 21st century unless you believe in oligarchy which is a caste system by which most of humanity is forced into penury with no chance of vertical mobility, a dissolution of privacy and free speech, constant wars on third world countries for corporate protection and profit, and theocracy as arbitrator of your morality. The good guys are no longer winning. The bills, statutes, laws, and taxes passed through Congress and the decisions adjudicated by the Supreme Court no longer have anything to do with PUBLIC good, only the greed of a few individuals and the hatred of a few others. Hunter Thompson reminded us of how things were supposed to be not how they are currently.

What is planted and cultivated in a society, like a garden, grows there. I didn't make that up. It's a fact. If you plant corn, roses will not grow from the seeds. If you hoe away the corn, weeds will thrive in the fertile soil. Do you ever think about the Italian Renaissance? I do, especially if I exchange my Prozac for cheap whiskey. Michelangelo, Da Vinci, Donatello, Bellini, Titian, Botticelli, Caravaggio, Ghiberti, Giotto, and Raphael are only a few of the artists who have influenced the world of art for the last six hundred years, and they all came from a tiny nation that boasted a population of less than ten million people. Why? Because what is planted and cultivated in a society grows there. During this era in Italian history, art was planted in every child's mind. When that child was old enough, he was propped in front of a canvas, paintbrush in hand. Art was cultivated.

Here's what we've done as a nation for the last century, or so: planted idiots in Congress and then not weeded them out in new elections. In the days of old when true public servants existed, they happened to be men who considered holding elective office a responsibility that went along with the rewards of living here, not an entry level job to gain experience for corporate lobbying. They had their own professions or were retired with wealth already. While corruption certainly existed, there were always those men in Congress who had enough integrity and backbone to work for the public trust. That kept the Republic fluid and functioning. Serving as congressmen was a way to give back to society which, in turn, produced an environment conducive to their past successes in the private sector. Think about the beginning of the 19th century. The population of this country was around two million. History offers us the biographies of men such as Washington, Adams, Franklin, Burr, Madison, Hancock, and Jefferson, among others. These were not perfect men. They had flaws, but the contract they lived by was a *social* contract with Jean-Jacques Rousseau instead of a business arrangement with Jeff Bezos or Elon Musk. Today in a country with three hundred million people, it is no longer possible to name even one statesman with their integrity and self-sacrificing spirit. Those days, and for the most part that caliber of politician, have long since departed.

The shift in direction began to occur when men came to see national politics as a career instead of a privileged duty and when statesmanship was no longer planted in our little democratic garden. Politicians *needed* re-election at all costs to make a living both during their political years and after without ever doing much in the way of actual work. I'm making a guess here without substantiation that this change of attitude and direction began to grow during the Industrial Revolution in the 19th century at a time when men such as Vanderbilt, Carnegie, Rockefeller, and J.P Morgan threw around boxcars full of money in Washington, D.C. to influence public policy. For senators and congressmen to be re-elected, these self-centered assholes had to forge relationships with private entities—banks, corporations, military contractors, and local companies that seek power and influence over everything from interest rates to interstate commerce to international wars.

Whenever it started, it's impossible to deny the current existence of a widespread sleaze in our capital now, especially since the Supreme Court decided that corporations are people for the purpose of buying elections. If elected officials owe their livelihood to special interests, then they choose frequently to vote in a manner consistent with those short term and local interests to protect that livelihood.

The shift in priorities I'm talking about marked the beginning of the end of a young democracy. Some governing still got done through the process Thompson describes as Argument as late in our history as a two or three decades ago. From each end of the left/right ideological spectrum politicians quarreled, squabbled, and bickered until a few decent humans on both sides realized the opposition held some notions that were mutually beneficial and would elevate the quality of life for most people in the country. Since representation was the essence of their job description and since their egos struggled to avoid embarrassment at all costs, they often reached solid ground somewhere around the middle of an issue.

But, as Hunter discerns, arguments of principal can only evolve into arguments of practicality when the people doing the screaming are capable of reason, of enough humility and common sense and compassion to accept the possibility that our entire collective society should not be relegated to their individual selfish whims. The Rogerian method of argument based on the belief that winners take all doesn't have to be the result of every disagreement has allowed this country to operate relatively well, or at least manage.

All of what you have now read would have remained an internal rant spurred into my thought processes by reflecting on Hunter Thompson's words had I not gotten out of bed to pour another shot of good Kentucky bourbon purchased with my race innings—a synthesis of desire and economic power. Did you know you can buy a bottle of ten-year-old Ancient Age for eighteen dollars, and it tastes better than most forty-dollar bottles?

The bourbon rested on a cheap wooden desk in the motel room next to the tiny single cup Mr. Coffee—what other company specializes in appliances for dwarfs—two free tea bags, Styrofoam cups stacked neatly next to the enveloped sugar and powdered cream substitutes, a red swizzle stick, a broken lamp, and a tourist brochure – "Visit Henry Clay's Home in Lexington, Tours Daily."

A vague flame of memory began to burn. Henry Clay had never come up in a single conversation with anyone in my life other than comments forced from me by Arawanna Huey who was my sixth-grade social studies teacher. Arawanna had been blessed with a stern Pentecostal upbringing. Moreover, she truly believed that the discipline required to memorize historical trivia would help us and so applied a torrent of threats to a study of Mr. Clay and other political figures from the ancient world of America that existed before there was ever baseball and girls.

In those days, I felt that Mrs. Huey simply pulled her hair into a bun so tightly each morning that she cut off circulation in her brain. Yet here in my old age sitting at a scarred desk in a cheap motel half-drunk from whiskey and contemplating the depraved mess that we laughingly call politics, I saw method in her madness. With his name of that brochure, Henry's info came roaring back in all its glory. Mrs. Huey was an underappreciated pedagogical genius, and Clay was an oxymoron, an almost honest lawyer. He developed great speaking ability in the courtrooms of Lexington, Kentucky.

After becoming a wealthy landowner because of the clients he fleeced, Clay went on to serve his country in both the House of Representatives and the Senate before being elevated to Secretary of State under John Quincy Adams. His fight for increased tariffs created the foundation for American supremacy in the industrial world. He maintained the idea that federal tax money collected from ALL citizens should be used to support society's infrastructure (i.e. roads, schools, hospitals), and Clay opposed the annexation of Texas. In the 21st century it's easy to see the farsighted wisdom of that latter notion. Henry Clay is now recognized as one of the five greatest senators in American history and best of all, Abraham Lincoln liked him. That's a pretty good recommendation for anybody.

Most importantly for me, on this evening of whiskey swilling, Hunter Thompson, KFC, racetrack success, and the constant barrage of bad news about our broken system of government that dominates every type of news disseminating media 24/7, was Clay's famous nickname, The Great Compromiser. Based on his wisdom and a belief that everyone, including and especially Congress, was responsible for the public welfare, he brokered famous agreements across party lines such as the Missouri Compromise of 1820, the Compromise of 1850, The Nullification

Crisis, and several others on the issue of slavery that not only kept the Union together but made life better for most of our people. His work moved us closer to the eventual elimination of white people owning black people.

This primary quality of compromise as a statesman of great virtue is the very same quality many politicians, wealthy conservatives, and war mongering Jesus-freak evangelicals called Christian Nationalists, view as anathema to their ideal of a perfect society, which is a frightening form of theological and economical fascism.

And that's when it hit me, this great idea formed from a synthesis churning around in my alcohol-addled brain. Why don't our representatives in Washington, D.C. sit down together and do the job they were elected to do instead of fucking each other and the rest of us to make a crooked buck? Maybe, it's the thrill of being above the law because you create the law. Forty-plus years ago when I was training racehorses myself here in Kentucky, I knew a veterinarian who was a world-class equine surgeon. He traveled first class everywhere to operate on some of the best racehorses ever bred. A genius, he formulated his own brand of leg medicines and had a medical practice worth millions of dollars. If you believe in clichés, the world was his oyster. But Doc owned a few racehorses himself, and he loved to gamble. He had no problem risking his vet license and possibly even jail to drug said horses illegally in hopes of winning a big bet. I asked him once why he did that considering he already had all the money anybody could ever need. His simple and yet complicated reply – "Because every dollar I can make dishonestly is more exciting and fun and easier than every hundred dollars I can make legally."

While it may be his logic applies to some congressmen, it doesn't work for me. Life isn't a horse race, even metaphorically. Everything is not about winning. Congress exists primarily to levy taxes and institute laws that allow most people in our society to benefit. Politicians are not elected to line their own pockets, force people to adhere to one religious code, or surrender the responsibility of governing to multi-national corporations that exist in an amoral vacuum.

I know it's unheard of these days to argue passionately for a problem-solving solution to a situation that concerns the entire population and at the same time be reasonable enough to surrender elements of that solution when someone on the opposite side shows you a more beneficial way. I realize that facts no longer matter in debate if your own interests suffer from their inclusion in the conversation. On the other hand, stupidity only goes so far before the natural world is forced to correct itself, and I believe we are approaching the outer limits of nature's patience regarding collective living, environmental concerns, technological advancements with no ethical restraints, human greed, and religious arrogance. Soon, the planet will need to start over, maybe without humans.

Is this outcome inevitable? I don't know. Synthesis thinking is not the same as prophetic insight. It's more like common sense. Here's what I do know. Compromise is not a novel concept. As a matter of fact, it is a proven means of solving a lot of the issues we currently claim are irresolvable. Our problem stems from an unwillingness to synthesize ideas from the extreme right and left edges of our ideological differences into answers that rise from the middle and become greater than the sum of their fanatical parts. How we go about cultivating an attitude of compromise for the greater good in our 21st century politicians is a difficult question. But, if I'm right that what grows in a garden relates directly to what is planted and cultivated there, maybe we need teachers like Arawanna Huey to conduct social studies classes in Washington, D. C.

Let's Consider Context – Education

It's a quiet day in the classroom. The children are indifferent to the lesson. Some have heard similar concepts earlier in their academic careers and some have not. Nevertheless, it's impossible for me to go forward with the course guidelines unless I first establish a baseline from which to proceed. I continue.

"In the English language, or Standard English as written, what two things must a sentence contain to be considered complete?"

There is a long pause – actually a few seconds, it just feels longer with twenty-five fresh, young faces imploring you to help them as if they were drowning puppies. Finally, one hand rises tentatively, is withdrawn, and rises again.

"Yes, Rachel?"

"Would that be a period and a capital letter?"

"Great guess," I respond. "What year did you get out of the first grade?"

If my response to Rachel's response seems a bit caustic, it's probably because I've been doing this for years and each year things get worse. Oh, did I forget to mention that these are college freshmen. I never taught at an Ivy League school, but even so I might be justified in expecting an answer something like "subject and verb" or "subject and predicate" or any damn thing similar. Sadly, I receive these kinds of comments frequently from young adults recently graduated from high school. "Do you know where Montreal is?" "I think it might be a country somewhere close to Canada." "When was the Civil War fought?" "1955, and thank you for your service in that war, Mr. McGarrah." "Has anyone heard of T.S. Eliot?" "Yeah, he plays bass in Johnny Cash's band."

Every one of these examples is an accurate call and response from one of my classes at some point in the last ten years, not some hyperbolic fantasy from a hysterical liberal. And, these are only a few.

My friend, Gary Hamer, sent me a tee shirt that reads *Ever Feel Like You're One Dumb Ass Away from Losing It?* He sent it to me for a reason. He understands the world people our age live in. Are students really becoming more stupid? The answer is unequivocally – NO. They are being taught less, intellectually challenged less. Less is required and less is expected. We blame it on technology. We blame it on some kind of attention deficit disorder, power lines, vaccinations, GMO's, sugar, single-parent families, music, or liberals. But the bottom line is not so complex. Less is required. Here are examples from the test public education students in the eighth grade needed to pass before entering high school in Salina, Kansas, during the 1895 school year:

1. Give the nine rules for the use of Capital Letters.

2. Name the parts of speech and define those that have no modifications.

3. Define: Verse, Stanza and Paragraph.

4. What are the principal parts of a verb? Give the Principal Parts of do, lie, lay, and run.

5. Define Case. Illustrate each case.

6. What is Punctuation? Give rules for principal marks of punctuation.

7-10. Write a composition of about 150 words and show therein that you understand the practical use of the rules of grammar.

These questions are from the English section of the test. Literature, Creative Writing and Composition, are subjects I teach for the English department. Were I to give this test to incoming college freshmen tomorrow, many, if not all, would fail. You may argue, and some do, that this knowledge is no longer relevant. I would reply that, given the state of the world, communication is very relevant and greatly needed. Would you eat an expensive gourmet meal with forks, knives, and plates? You know, just dump all the crap together in a big pile and stuff it in your mouth without regard to taste, or manners, or the clarity of the ingredients. If you were a hog and not a human, yes. Otherwise, no. Why don't exquisite and important ideas deserve the same respect as a good meal? Organize, structure, clarify, and unify are all jobs of grammar. Like eating utensils, they may not be the most important part of a meal, but they certainly enhance it.

1. Give the epochs into which U.S. History is divided.

2. Give an account of the discovery of America by Columbus.

3. Relate the causes and results of the Revolutionary War.

4. Show the territorial growth of the United States.

5. Tell what you can of the history of Kansas.

6. Describe three of the most prominent battles of the Rebellion.

7. Who were the following: Morse, Whitney, Fulton, Bell, Lincoln, Penn and Howe?

8. Name the events connected with the following dates: 1607, 1620, 1800, 1849 and 1865.

The basic idea behind a representative form of government, a democracy, is the concept of an educated citizenry. The questions above stem from the History section of that same 1895 eighth grade test in Salina, Kansas. I have never met a college freshman in the 21st Century who could answer them. Here's another example of how dumb we've become from a recent blog article by Gary Bentley. "In 2011, Newsweek asked 1,000 Americans to take the standard U.S. Citizenship test, and 38 percent of them failed. One in three couldn't name the vice-president."

Our democracy is currently broken. How can it be repaired any more than any other engine if the mechanics have no idea how it was built and how it operates? I won't bore you with the other sections from this test. I sure as hell couldn't pass the math section myself. But it does raise another question for me personally. Who wants the American people so dumbed down? Sadly, the answer may be the American people, and thanks to the Supreme Court, that includes corporations now, especially corporations.

Most of us will spend our lives as part of a gigantic workforce. Call us worker bees, drones, whatever you want, that is the reality. We will punch a time clock and fill some kind of quota. Some will be paid better than others. Some will be happier than others doing their jobs, but the work will still be a job. We get up, commute, function as automatons for eight or nine hours, commute home, watch TV, eat dinner, sleep, and start the same process over the next day, five days a week for three or four decades. If we're lucky, we'll live long enough to enjoy a small pension unless the people we work for have stolen it. A gifted and lucky few get to have careers, something better than a job because they like doing what they do to earn a living. This struggle to find a life in the midst of banality has taken a tangible form called materialism. We equate happiness with earning power and in so doing, demand education be geared to achieve that end and only that end. Employers appreciate this attitude because the result is a compliant workforce that neither questions nor demands.

Our current culture leaves a traditional university education and the universities that provide it scuffling with technical colleges and trade schools, attempting to fulfill a mission they were not designed to bother with in the 17th, 18th,19th, and 20th centuries. University administrators must convince prospective students and their parents that attending the classes available translates into earning power. A university education is more expensive now than it ever has been and more than it should be, not because the faculty is well paid, but rather because business-oriented administrators are overpaid, along with coaches. New buildings are built to enhance the appearance of the campus. Textbooks—way overpriced to begin with—usually last only one or two semesters. The textbook companies then provide a new *edition*, which is the same as the old one with some minor changes and a higher cost, and the student must buy into the monopoly to take the class. Like a lot of *products* in our capitalistic society, the cost has risen far above the ability of working Americans to pay. For students and their parents, this process is like the old company store cycle created by mining companies in the early twentieth century. The difference being that higher education is still a matter of choice.

In order for people to borrow tens of thousands of dollars, make this sacrifice, and accept this paradigm, they must believe their choice will be access to a high paying job, not simply the ability to think critically, communicate, converse, show compassion, learn respect for intelligence, and accept the responsibility for self-governance, which have always been the objectives of an undergraduate university education since the model was invented by ancient Greece. Universities must offer tangible material results now if they are to stay in business and compete with tech schools. People must feel that their children can leave a four-year undergraduate education with a trade, or access to one. Parents send their kids to school as clients, or customers, not students. They want a usable product in return.

This new direction begins in the lower grades, especially in high schools. States are moving away from reading literature in high school. The go to assignments these days come from technical catalogues. Who needs Shakespeare, Orwell, Melville, Eliot, or Swift in order to go punch a time clock? Why study philosophy when tests are standardized and require no critical thought or logical ability? No one needs to look at a Picasso or Rembrandt to spray paint a car fender on an assembly line or push a button so a robot does it.

I'm not making an argument here that work of this nature is

unimportant. It's vital to any thriving economy if it is to remain a surviving economy. The point is more nuanced. I'm saying that a liberal arts education elevates the humans who do this kind, and every other kind, of work. Education in the humanities makes people better humans because they think and are willing to evolve intellectually and emotionally. This does not necessarily follow that it makes them more compliant workers. In many cases, the opposite is true. That's the problem for the employing elite in this country. Educated people ask too many questions, can provide historical and ethical references for raises and better working conditions, realize that a job is not a life, and they are able to prioritize rather than follow orders blindly. What I'm saying and what I believe has more to do with the creation of possibilities for bettering the conditions of all rather than increasing the wealth of a few.

"Dumbing Down" is a clichéd term now. Unfortunately, it has become an expectation, almost positive in its application. There's nothing new or profound in what I've stated in the last few paragraphs. I'm no great thinker. I have no dog in this hunt, so to speak. My children are adults, educated in the humanities and working good jobs as well. One is not mutually exclusive from the other. I guess that's my point. It isn't necessary or even profitable in the long run to make it that way. As a matter of fact, I believe it's dangerous.

Synonyms Are Not Antonyms (Hint: this note is not a grammar lesson)

In an ancient time, the 1950's to be precise, I was a student at Lowell Elementary School in the southern Indiana town of Princeton. My boyhood wasn't much different than many white, middle-class Midwestern boys. I played Little League baseball, watched Zorro and Gunsmoke and Howdy Doody on a black and white television and did very little actual thinking. I was denied almost nothing in the way of material things. My parents were affectionate, decent, upper middle-class people. I rode my Schwinn three-speed bicycle around town safely, walked to school, and never knew a locked door.

One of my favorite games played at recess during the school year consisted of drawing a circle in the playground dirt at recess. Two or three of us would dump our collections of glass marbles, a shiny, multi-colored handful of ball bearing sized objects. Placing one of the marbles we held back between our thumbs and first finger, we flicked the marble into the circle with the hope of knocking one of the other marbles outside the boundary of the ring. We took turns one at a time until all the marbles had been gathered. The boy who had the most won the game, which we labeled *Keepsies,* and sometimes *War.* The winner bagged his trophies.

This was the object of the game. There was no other. You simply became marble rich or marble poor, and your status in schoolyard society was precipitated on who had the largest bag full of marbles. They were our currency. We could trade them, buy influence with them, or own them and be wealthy. Some boys would cheat and fudge the boundaries or move the pieces when no one looked. Some would bully other players. Our only goal was to get more marbles. I didn't understand what the game was helping us to learn at the time. It was fun. That's all. But the lesson became apparent as I grew into adulthood. The game of marbles has become the main motivating force of our whole society, especially in the 21st century. It drives everything from politics to medicine, even our system of higher education.

Greed. We don't call it that. We have a label that justifies greed as a normal and productive part of free society. In fact, it has become the essence of our lives. Capitalism is the name we bestow on this phenomenon, but it is more than that. To be considered a winner in America, the only principle you need to live by is playing for "all the marbles." There are many problems with that attitude. The main one is confusing greed and capitalism. They are not synonyms. The words cannot be interchanged equally. Simply by voicing this opinion, I will be labeled by some as a communist.

One reason the notion of capitalism has become synonymous with greed in America lies in the effort put forth by huge corporations to make any other word not connected with buying and selling our way of life seem abhorrent to good hard-working Americans. Even the term liberal carries the same negative economic connotation as communist, socialist, serial killer, and welfare fraud. Just ask anyone who works for Fox News. The only words we are allowed to utter in polite society in relation to capitalism are these two—freedom and Jesus. Money in the bank is now the essence of both. "Follow the money" has become normalized in our daily lives as the agenda for almost everything we say and do collectively as a player on the world stage.

When we talk about exporting freedom to underdeveloped countries what we really mean is exporting our business interests for the collection of their natural resources. It simply sounds better to say our chief export is freedom. When we send troops to protect the interests of our corporations, we call them liberators. However, what the military liberates is usually quantifiable in terms of currency and resources rather than humanity. Don't take my word for it. Read some history. History is loaded with terrifying things called *facts*. These dream crushers that some people dare to use as evidence when describing certain events often create a dilemma for the greedy. I call it truth. For example, the truth is we have been in the business of war since the inception of our nation, and every war fought has generated huge profits for private American business interests. If that were not the case, our reticence in fighting them would be more apparent.

I'm not going to belabor this point. I'm not writing an academic article. I'm sharing my opinion of what's already common knowledge for those who seek it. If you desire to fact-check what you read here, I urge you to do it. It's probably time we researched something other than football scores anyway. With that said, here are some brief examples that come to my mind that I have personally lived through. Remember the first Gulf War. We fought that war to liberate the people of Kuwait from Saddam Hussein's occupying army. It was the humanitarian thing to do. Forget the fact that Kuwait is incredibly oil rich and Exxon, Shell, and British Petroleum, among other corporations have huge investments there. We just wanted to bring freedom to the Kuwaiti people. And we did. Sort of. We kicked ole Saddam clean out of there and thirty years later that tiny country is still ruled by the same corporate-friendly autocratic dictators they have always been. Unfortunately, the oil became no freer than the common people.

Meanwhile, during that same decade Rwanda suffered through genocidal horrors. Croatia and Bosnia fell victims to ethnic cleansing by barbaric Serbian paramilitary factions. However, we couldn't aid those beleaguered countries because we didn't want to interfere with another nation's sovereignty. As it turns out, this proved to be code for *they have nothing we want.* Finally, a decade late and pressured by the rest of the world, we did exercise a bombing campaign in Kosovo that helped bring the "ethnic cleansing" to an end. How about that dirty Taliban in Afghanistan? Well, we fought them for the first two decades of the 21st century, but we also put them in power and armed them during the decade of the 1980's to fight the Soviets and protect our oil pipelines through the Middle East. At the time, that effort got sold to the

American public as a means to protect an Afghan democracy from communism. Ask any woman in that country today how much freedom she has under Taliban rule, especially those school-age girls whose faces have been burned off with acid for trying to get an education.

I'll just pile another soapbox on top of my soapbox. Is there anyone out there old enough to remember Latin America in the 1970's? Salvadore Allende happened to be Chile's first *democratically* elected president. He was a good man, an honest man by all historical accounts. But he had a big flaw. Allende believed in socialism. Just as he seemed about ready to confiscate the American corporations raping his country for the benefit of his enslaved people and move his economy away from dependence on the crumbs left by American corporations, he was assassinated, and a coup took place. With the help of the CIA, General Augusto Pinochet saved Chile for freedom and Jesus. Of course, thirty some years later Pinochet stood convicted of crimes against humanity, but as far as I know American business interests are making grand profits in Chile.

Chile is one example in Latin America from the seventies. Guatemala, Ecuador, Nicaragua, and Panama also spring to mind. No example is more telling than when the movie star of *Bedtime for Bonzo*, Ronald Reagan, decided to invade the terrible socialist country of Grenada—the population of the entire country is somewhat less than a small American city—to protect 800 American students who were trapped on the island. Incidentally, when questioned 90% of said students admitted they did not want to be evacuated and were not trapped because charter flights left the island on a regular basis. We conquered our enemy within a few weeks and Reagan was a hero with only a few dead Americans to worry about. Like Iraq in the 21st century, the public had been grievously misled in the name of Capitalism. Here's what the Global Policy Forum had to say about that invasion:

Grenada's foreign policy was not subservient to the American government. Many believe that Grenada was seen as a bad example for other poor Caribbean states. Its economy dominated by U.S. corporate interests. A show of force would cause states with similar leftist nationalist ideals to think twice. If a country as small and poor as Grenada could have continued its rapid rate of development under a socialist model, it would set a bad precedent for other Third World countries. In short, Grenada under the New Jewel Movement was reaching a dangerous level of health care, literacy, housing, participatory democracy, and economic independence.

If I jump to the sixties, I have a very personal memory of capitalism fighting to bring democracy to a third world country rich in natural resources and geographically strategic. This country was called Vietnam. American corporations made and are still making a fortune in Southeast Asia the same way some of those same companies have made a fortune in Iraq during the first decade of the 21st century. I could go on and on and on recounting our foreign affairs history decade by decade all the way back to 1790. What normally motivates the foreign policy of our government can be traced directly to what best serves our business interests. In other words, we may have never been a democracy at all but rather an oligarchy content to sacrifice our young to the gods of war in return for profit. What was supposed to drive the engine of our new radical form of representative government, the implementation of a free market economy, ironically, may have been what has always governed us and thus prevented that real democratic way of life. What about Ukraine? We seem to be doing the noble thing there, and I agree with supporting the effort to stop Russia. However, we have no foot soldiers on the ground there yet, but who is our government buying the weapons from that we send to aid Ukrainians? Who is profiting?

I'm not only referring to our relationships with other countries. We are told by politicians who rely on corporate lobbying money for their livelihood that everyone wants to come to America because we have it better here than anywhere else in the world. This is true, but only for some people. Over forty million citizens here go without any type of health care. Why? Because it isn't profitable for health insurance companies to cover them. Our public education system continues a downward spiral, and what once was a model for the world has become a joke. Why? Because the tax dollars that should be supporting it are constantly diverted to support political pork barrel projects, including private schools. The conservative view seems to be that when public schools fail, they can be replaced by a private, for-profit, educational system. Of course, when that happens the quality of education for students will no longer matter as much as the profits generated by their presence. A free-market school system will also allow the closing of schools in unprofitable impoverished areas. But hey, poor kids don't need to know anything but how to punch a time clock anyway.

Our state and federal prisons have become obsolete. Why? Because they are not making money. We are in the process of privatizing that system, which means that prisons can no longer operate at a loss as part of societal responsibility. You must keep the cells full so the new prison corporations can pay their shareholders' dividends. Because of that need, state run mental hospitals closed their doors and shifted their populations to private prisons. Now, people who suffer from repairable disorders get housed with violent sociopaths. Young men and women convicted of minor drug offenses receive unconscionable sentences of up to life in prison, especially if they are part of an ethnic minority demographic.

Every developed country in the world has a certain segment of its citizenry that live under bridges, in abandoned warehouses, or under trees in city parks. For the most part, these are indigents, drug addicts, refugees from war torn areas, and teenage runaways. According to *The Economist,* 12,000 homeless roam Parisian streets every night. Most of them are North African males who are refugees from famine-ridden countries. A quick tour of google.com will tell the discerning researcher that 50,000 people live without homes in New York and 20,000 of them are children. That figure rises exponentially in warmer climates of the

U.S. Every night 3.5 million people sleep wherever they can find a place to lie down. 1.5 million are children. The number of homeless children in this country seems so disproportionate because of subprime lending. We turn families out for profit. They have no homes. Those homes were foreclosed on so Wall Street bankers would not lose their investments.

I could continue this argument *ad infinitum.* There's plenty more to say. But, if you're not listening now, more won't help you. The bottom line is simple. Economic theories are not political and social philosophies. Corporations are amoral. They exist for profit and profit only. They have and always will play "keepsies" with us for all the marbles. They have no democratic value systems to guide them. There is little compassion or empathy built into the banking system or ethical protection into Wall Street, even the regulations are rarely enforced. If America doesn't begin to restructure its priorities soon, we will be way beyond the vanishing point, that speck on the horizon where this oligarchic sky over us plunges into a sea of angry humanity and whatever's left of what we thought was an American Dream disappears forever.

Economic solutions exist. They have always existed. The problem lies in our reticence to implement them because they cost tax money. It's an attitude thing we are suffering from, not a lack of good ideas. Instead of cutting back on humanities programs in favor of technical programs, universities need to expand them. The first and foremost obligation of any university should be training a new generation in critical thinking and citizenship responsibility, not teaching a trade online because it's more profit oriented to do so. Sabbatical leaves for factory workers who wish to engage in community activity such as Habitat for Humanity could be offered to people with seniority in their jobs. CEO salaries at major corporations and financial institutions might be restricted to a certain percentage of employee salaries and thus reduce the incentive for corruption. Lobbyists could be banned from Congress and the Citizens United Law overturned. Tax loopholes for the wealthy could be closed and the revenue gain applied to social programs. War as an instrument of foreign policy and for the protection of corporate interest abroad must be eliminated. Putin has started one in the Ukraine this time, instead of Biden somewhere. We are giving Ukraine necessary support. Our effort is to be applauded in that regard. However, try to remember that what we give them, we bought from corporate defense contractors who will end up being the big winners, not Ukraine.

There are hundreds of good ideas already on the table that would bring America back from the ethical abyss. Why don't we institute some of them? The answer is both simple and incredibly complex. We will never be able to change the direction of society without first raising the consciousness of the individuals who make it up and urging ourselves and our neighbors, on our own, to establish priorities that have less to do with wealth and more to do with each other. Can all our problems be solved? Of course not. Democracy is not utopia. But democracy is about more than who has all the marbles.

"Don't Sweat the Small Stuff"

A few years ago, I lived in an apartment complex not far from the University of Georgia in Athens about fifty miles from Atlanta. It's a fine place with tree-line boulevards, landscapers constantly mowing-trimming-raking-planting, a small lake with a resident flock of geese, and wrought iron gates in and out that must be opened with a code. The gates, however, are more pretention than practical, a fact in evidence as you watch the Domino's Pizza delivery man drive in unrestrained.

The apartment complex is owned by a shadowy corporation headquartered somewhere in California. This LLC group owns like properties all over the United States. That many holdings require another corporation that specializes in "property management" as overseers. They in turn hire people to run the complexes onsite for leasing and maintenance. Each of these groups has their own company name. Every time the big boss corporation—remember, corporations are people now—decides to add investors or do something stock related, it requires level number two to make sure all documents at each individual complex are correct and up to date.

Now, you know where this is going because all of you have dealt at some time in your lives with the surrealistic and apocalyptic nonsense generated by the bottom dweller bureaucrats in this scenario. They are the poor bastards who work at each individual complex for the short adrenalin bursts of power handed them like a sacramental host, the barely competent, and often petty managers onsite in any similar situation—the local managers of Walmart, Kroger's, the local license bureau, the Dollar Store, Home Depot, Hobby Lobby, McDonalds, etc.

At the scent of an upper management inspection panic invades their tiny offices as the minions search for every document required and seek out each undotted i or uncrossed t that renders the document invalid or, at worst, against some rule arbitrarily composed at the level above in this bureaucratic labyrinth of lost souls. It has nothing to do with efficiency or customer satisfaction or common sense and everything to do with what I call the "cover-your-own-ass" syndrome.

My apartment home gets one of these inspections three or four times a year. We have one next week. Tenants have been forewarned by email that all things must be up to code and management would be checking our documents again. I had lived here for just over three years. When I moved in all my documents were received at the office and poured over succinctly by the staff and judged to be in order. Nothing has changed about necessary paperwork in these three years. But staff has come and gone, and every time the person in charge of insurance forms changes, I get a phone call. Each phone call is the same.

"Mr. McGarrah, we don't have your insurance form."

"Yes, you do."

"No, we don't and you must get it to us ASAP."

"Okay, I'll bring you another copy. Try to hold on to this one."

Yesterday, I received a call from a new staff member per upcoming inspection. "Mr. McGarrah, we don't have your insurance form." I must admit that my reply may have been less than polite, snippy even, to which I received a snip in return.

"Sir, I don't like the attitude you're giving me."

"I don't like to be bothered for a form I've personally placed in your office three times in the past year."

"It's a petty matter, sir. There's no reason for that tone."

"It's not petty if you're driving me insane with your inability to hold on to a piece of paper. This is a waste of my time *again* and at my age I haven't got any time to spare for nonsense."

Tact and patience are qualities that I should have done better cultivating but didn't. I know this, and I acquiesced to his demand reluctantly. I took the original document from my files, walked across the parking lot, and entered the leasing office.

"I brought you the original. Now, I want to see you make a copy and place it in my file so we never have to do this again. State Farm sends you an automatic renewal every year. It's specified right there on the policy."

At that point it became apparent that we would never be close friends. He clutched the document to his chest and went to the copy machine.

"Well, here's the problem," he said, strutting back into the room. "Where it says *additional interests,* the address is wrong. State Farm has listed this apartment complex."

"Yes. That's where I live."

"It has to say our parent company's name."

My head almost exploded. Fortunately, I had drunk my morning coffee already and was able to restrain myself, which is why I am able to relate this memory from my home and not a maximum-security prison.

"You mean to tell me that all these times the problem was a misprinted address on the form you had and not the fact that you didn't have the form? You realize that I could have turned in a hundred more copies with the same misprint and never known how to correct this."

"Unfortunately, it seems so, but we'll fix it right this time."

This situation is, of course, petty nonsense in a world of plagues, wars, famine, wildfires, and Republican politicians. However, it does illustrate a salient point. The angrier the world becomes, the more difficult it seems to be for people to communicate accurately and reasonably with each other. This in turn raises the heat of the moment, which can then cascade into major anxiety for everyone involved and sometimes beyond. Did the fellow in Texas who shot up a Taco Bell because the server forgot his hot sauce expect it to be there and not ask for it? Who knows? But it was a petty miscommunication that led to a tragedy, and it hasn't been an isolated incident this year.

I guess there's no one specific reason why these tiny speed bumps on the road to peaceful living bother me, maybe a lot of us, so much. Do we rant and rave at the minor stuff because we have no control over the major stuff, and it provides some illusion of that last control? Are we miserable and misery loves company? Is it entitlement, arrogance, or delusions of self-importance? The answer may be any or all these things. Here's what I do know.

The anger I feel toward other people in many mundane situations usually comes from some slight miscommunication. I have not asked for exactly what I want and take for granted another person should know. Maybe I was distracted and heard only part of what was said. Maybe I expect too much from other people because I don't expect enough from myself. It's a complex issue that seems simple. I might never get the answer to it straight, and the point is exacerbated when the people I'm trying to communicate with are only halfway listening or halfway answering. That's okay, though, if I can apply the lesson my father always tried to teach me, and I'm trying too even if it sometimes requires more empathy than I can muster or more humility than I ordinarily show.

My father applied this rule for dealing with other people and maintaining balance himself. "Don't sweat the small stuff. It's the tiny inconveniences that eat us up inside if we let them because we try and ignore the stuff that overwhelms us. Things that mean very little in the grand scheme of life often make us the most miserable. Don't let them." I think this is pretty good advice for our current way of life.

The Truth about Mangoes

Shelagh Shapiro will do an interview with me in a few weeks on her radio show *Write the Book*. One of the subjects we will probably discuss is the significance of the title for my newest collection of poems. *The Truth about Mangoes* is an odd one to be sure. Like most writers of poetry and fiction and creative nonfiction, I don't start my poems and essays with a theme in mind. I start with a story or an event or a memory that won't let me be alone and try to share that as clearly and meaningfully as possible. My work becomes a translation of sorts, and what I translate is human experience into words, often with the inherent bias of my personal perspective. The unifying or dominant idea that threads its way through the work is developed by the telling itself. A pattern emerges that becomes recognizable and shared by readers. I guess this forms what critics and scholars call themes in literature, a motif that is relatable whether they experience it themselves or not.

Certainly, that seems the case with *The Truth about Mangoes*, a single poem that began with the memory of a frequent argument between my mother and me. Our disagreements were rare, almost nonexistent, not because I was a reasonable person and not because I lacked confidence in my opinions as a young man. It had more to do with my mother's personality. She was physically beautiful, demure, and even aloof at times. Her moral compass pointed toward sobriety, integrity, and loyalty as well as an inherent goodness and an empathy for all God's creatures. She would not raise her voice, nor would she engage in a protracted disagreement over politics, religion, sexual mores, or my father's gin drinking. Things were what they were, and she handled each circumstance with a stoic resignation common to women of her Post World War II generation, except for the subject of green bell peppers.

In rural southern Indiana as a child, I never heard bell peppers called anything but mangoes. If my mother stuffed them with rice, diced them for chili, sliced them for salads, or sautéed them with sausages, they were mangoes. When she shopped at the grocery store, she would ask for fresh mangoes and be directed to a produce section full of bell peppers by the clerk. If we visited one of her friends for lunch, we all ate mangoes. This remained a constant in my life until I left home at the age of eighteen. I was at a restaurant somewhere with a buddy who happened to order stuffed peppers. When they arrived, I said, "Those aren't peppers. They're mangoes." He replied, "Are you fucking crazy?" We argued considerably over the next half hour or so and then went our separate ways. I must confess that I was disturbed by his stupidity.

Over the next several years, I traveled the world courtesy of the military and ultimately my immersion in a nomadic hippie lifestyle immediately after my discharge from the Marine Corps in 1969. The subject of peppers had never become a focus of my conversations again until I found myself on Stock Island near Key West, Florida, snorkeling one spring in the early 1970's. Three of us had set up a tent on a sandy beach near a tangle of scruffy shrubs. Their roots were more like stilts holding them above the water in loose sand.

"What are those?" I asked a guy named Mike who was our resident trivia expert.

"They're mangroves."

"Mangroves as in mangoes?"

"Yeah, except these Florida bushes don't grow the real fruit. There's about eighty different types of mango trees and the best fruit comes from Southeast Asia. Weren't you just in Vietnam?"

"Yeah, but I wasn't paying a lot of attention to vegetation, except as concealment."

"You should've tried one. They're excellent."

"My mom stuffs them with hamburger and rice," I said.

Mike wrinkled his nose and rolled a joint. "She does what?"

"Stuffs them."

"Those are bell peppers, you fucking lunatic, not mangoes."

As it turns out, Mike was correct. One of my childhood delusions shattered on the spot, like many did during the nineteen sixties and seventies. But it was also the beginning of a constant, albeit minor, conflict with a woman whom I dearly loved and who went out of her way to never have a conflict with anyone. On my next trip home, I began trying to convince her that what she stuffed was a bell pepper. I made absolutely no progress on this point for the next thirty years.

I realized something as I worked on this poem and from that realization other poems grew. What I understood wasn't particularly profound and was something that I had probably known instinctively all along. But that's the great thing about poetry. It often reminds us of important aspects of the human condition that we never take time to examine ordinarily, and if you believe Socrates, an unexamined life isn't worth living. Each of us in our own way does exactly what my mother did. We assign value to objects and ideas based on our perspective and through that emphasis create our reality. That reality doesn't have to be real; however, and therein lies the difficulty we often create for ourselves. Imagine if my mother had made a mango juice smoothie with bell peppers or stuffed peppers with a mango. The result would be a *bad* tasting concoction that no one could enjoy. Now, imagine further that my mother never acknowledged this and forced her recipe on us at every opportunity.

We see the world as we want it to be or think it must be. In many instances, this is a benign trait and one that comes with free will and the ability to choose. In some cases, it even makes the world a better place. But often, the external reality conflicts violently with the internal reality we've created and while those encounters make for good dramatic writing in both poems and stories, they can also make for chaos and pain in actual life circumstances.

One of the great joys in creative writing is that we don't have to resolve those conflicts. We have omnipotent choices because we are the creators. A conflict can be resolved for the reader, and something learned, or a point reached where the reader realizes a conflict is unresolvable and—you guessed it—something learned. This makes for good literature, or what we like to label as art. On the other hand, if we refuse to recognize that in individual perspectives different realities often co-exist and attempt no reconciliation between them, we risk creating a work that is either too obscure or too fanciful for a willing suspension of disbelief. That makes for mediocre, even bad, literature.

Unconsciously, the poems in this new collection turned into an examination of that flaw in the human character—our inherent stubbornness to admit unpleasant facts or evidence that challenges our belief systems. It became a central motif running through them. As it is with many thematic issues it was an unconscious one that I didn't understand till I read the book. But it's one I hope readers will appreciate as well. It seems in this day and age that we've reached a point in society where we've become unwilling to change perspective, consider a bigger picture of reality than our own, to admit that something may not be real simply because it's our opinion or that opinion is not more important than facts in evidence. Agreeing that what we believe doesn't always have to be right, or even what is—a truth both terrifying and liberating at the same time—might allow us to raise living to the level of art. Or, if you want to quote Hemingway's last line in *The Sun Also Rises,* "Isn't it pretty to think so."

The Shill

On this hot night in the 21st century, a freckled girl connected to the hand of a future pig farmer bounced and floated like a helium balloon down the midway. Bittersweet smells from the melting cotton candy, burnt bearing grease, stale popcorn, and rotting caramel apples coated that same midway lit with neon bulbs and dim moonlight. The humidity remained constant and heavy on this last night of the Gibson County Fair, as it had for decades in the past and probably would for several decades forthcoming. The roadies tore down and packed up unused equipment. The thinning crowds moved slowly and purposefully. Some filtered out the main gate, arms laden with souvenirs and the remnants of extraordinary foods such as taffy, frozen hokey-pokeys, or the famous fairgrounds fish sandwich that would not reappear till the following summer. Others wandered in for a last glimpse of the side show freaks with garish limbs and hideous mutations or listened to the barely clothed hoochie-coochie girls painted like kewpie dolls as they hawked at old men to come in and watch them dance naked. The shaded spotlights shadowed perfectly their puffy, yellowing bodies and glazed-over eyes scarred by life.

As I passed the gambling tents, a greasy man wrinkled like leather and puffing between coughs on a cigarette waved me toward the bottle toss game. He juggled three baseballs in his hands and the cigarette bobbed between his thin lips in time with their rise and fall. A local teenager stacked milk bottles on a small stool behind him, and then the kid turned to smile. In that grin I saw my father, John Bill, during the summer of 1939.

John Bill paced the sawdust covered dirt in front of a three-sided canvas tent and rubbed two nickels together in his pocket for luck, a habit he carried with him all his life. Facing him, the open side of the tent beckoned. It was a long counter stacked with baseballs and behind the counter hanging from the walls, rows of bright, stuffed teddy bears, puppy dogs, and horses, along with shelves of costume jewelry and an odd assortment of whistles, badges, handcuffs, marbles, and balloons caught the eyes of passers-by. On the ground against the back canvas wall, two stools were stacked with five painted milk bottles each, three on the bottom row and two on the top.

The object seemed simple. You paid a nickel and the black-toothed carnie in a straw hat who stood next to the counter let you throw three baseballs. If you knocked over all the milk bottles, you could pick your prize.

My father was a star, a pitcher on his high school baseball team who would soon sign a contract with the St. Louis Cardinals. He felt desperate to win a stuffed animal. It was both a matter of athletic challenge and a way to impress my future mother Juanita, who was never easily impressed. Her current boyfriend happened to be Jim Peck, tall, well-to-do captain of the basketball team and honor student headed for Indiana University in the fall. But the two nickels in my father's pocket didn't belong to him. He had come to the fair on an errand. His mother, my grandmother, entrusted him with the little extra money available in their Depression era household to buy seeds at the Co-op stand that she could plant and turn into vegetables so the family might eat healthy meals during the coming winter. If dad lost her money and returned without those seeds, the result could prove a dietary and economic catastrophe with nothing to harvest and can, unless it was a stuffed animal.

The family, like many working-class families during the Great Depression, subsisted on almost nothing. My grandfather had labored for many years at the Southern Railway shop in Princeton, Indiana, repairing the great locomotives that hauled coal and grain out of the Midwest to both coasts. Since the Depression began, he faced one layoff after another, working only sporadically, earning barely enough to keep bread and beans on the table, a few lumps of coal in the stove, and an occasional block of ice in the ice box. My grandmother reduced her weekly dairy orders to *blue john*, milk with a pastel blue tint because the cream had been skimmed off the top and that tasted like water. This was their life and they all accepted it with a stoic resignation, but they all had to do their part, make sacrifices. The sacrifice making had always been the most difficult for my father. He didn't mind suffering, and he enjoyed hard work. What my dad hated all of his life was *deferred gratification.* He could barely stand to wait for something he wanted and believed he had earned, whether it was money, a woman, a drink, a house, a vacation, or a car. This itch, as he called it, required more scratching in his youth than when I knew him later in life. Of course, the infection passed from him to me. I know this because I've labored through four marriages, a dozen jobs, and several stages of penury believing that I deserve what I want before I've earned it and knowing a big score waits with the purchase of the next lottery ticket, the running of another race, a visit from the mailman, or the turn of a card. *The sins of the father*…you know the rest...are often multiplied by the son.

Beyond the economic concerns, a deeper and darker ethical gloom lurked in my father's mind, arising from fear, not only a legitimate anxiety created by his conscience but the absolute terror of getting on my grandmother's bad side. This ambivalence, the desire to gamble with money not his and the knowledge of his mother's strict disciplinary code if he did, caused him to shuffle and hesitate indecisively just long enough for the carnival huckster to beckon, "Hey you…yeah, you…the good looking ball player…the one standing there waiting to win yore girl a big ole cuddly bear…the one in bib overalls…the one who's gonna break my bank…come on over…be a real man…take a chance… . I got connections with a major league baseball scout, you know."

The hypnotic cadence of the man's baritone voice enhanced the decision my dad wanted to make anyway, and he found himself pulled, as if by some magic lasso to the carnie's counter.

"What do I have to do?" Dad asked.

"What's your name son?"

"John Bill."

"Well, John Bill, you ain't got much to do at all, not a big strappin' guy like you. You play ball?"

"I pitch for my high school team."

"I bet you're a good un, too."

"I win a lot of games."

It wasn't until much later in his life, after WWII, after years in the automobile business and after raising a half-crazed teenager that my father learned to fully dismiss bull shit. He worked hard for decades to give each stranger the benefit of the doubt until the world became so jaded around him he could no longer afford to do it. On this last night of the fair, he honestly believed that the man complimenting him was a nice man. Also, I'm sure that in the glare of the neon lights and the crooning of calliope music and his excited fantasies of Juanita, my future mother, he forgot his own mother's evangelical stringency about children obeying parents. She had always been a great advocate of the adage *spare the rod, spoil the child.* My father and his brother were not spoiled, as he could have attested to this last night of the fair had his memory not been numbed by his over stimulated senses and by the bright environment.

Once, and only once, Dad and Uncle Densil stole a chicken from Mr. Nixon's hen house a mile or so up the road in a neighborhood on the other side of the fairgrounds called Coal Mine Row. Their mother waited for them at the front door.

"Where'd that chicken come from?" She said, stepping out onto the porch.

"Densil won the spelling bee at school, and this was the prize."

"I see," she said. Moving forward, she took the chicken by the neck and twirled it over their heads, wringing the life from it before the poor bird sensed its impending doom. "Walter Nixon just rang on the telephone to tell me he saw you two boys stealing this here chicken."

"Oh no, that's not the way...," sputtered my uncle.

"Shut up. And git your overalls off. This chicken will be bought and paid for tomorrow because your father's going to spend his morning off work chopping a chord of wood for Walter for free. Meanwhile, your sister, your dad, and me are going to eat it for supper."

"What about us. We're hungry too."

"You won't be in a few minutes."

Both boys stripped down to their underwear. My grandmother reached behind the door and produced a willow switch. Smacking them across the calves in tandem, she ran them semi-nude into the field of razor-sharp nettle weeds that bordered her property.

"There won't be thieves and liars named McGarrah anywhere in this county."

Her voice could barely be heard above the screams of her sons. Dad and Uncle Densil went to their room without supper and nursed their bleeding legs. Imagine, if you can, a thousand paper cuts across your shins and thighs filled with itching, burning sap. In the 21st century my grandmother would be jailed for abuse and her children placed in foster care. As it turned out, my father grew up to be the most honest man I ever met, and at his funeral hundreds of people filled Colvin's Mortuary of Princeton, Indiana, to pay their respects for the same reason.

Unfortunately, that chicken theft and corresponding accountability escaped his mind as he placed the first nickel on the counter nervously and picked up three baseballs.

"Now John Bill, you got to knock all five bottles over. Do it on the first pitch and anything from the top row is yours."

With his eye on a huge black and white panda bear, Dad cocked his arm, went into his windup and let the ball fly. It whistled through the air and thudded, a direct hit, on the middle bottle, scooting it out from the two-on-top and three-on-bottom pyramid built by the man running the game. Instead, only that particular one toppled over, along with the one directly above it. Dad fired two more strikes and collapsed the other three bottles.

"You got a mighty fine throwing' arm, but it took you all three balls. You have to pick something from the bottom row."

"I don't understand. They all should've fallen with the first one."

"Sometimes life just ain't fair."

My father received a penny whistle for his five cents and started to leave.

"You ain't a quitter, are ya boy?"

"Not hardly."

"Well, there surely ain't no way the same bad break can happen twice."

Sometimes circumstance brings us to the edge of an abyss, a confluence of several events at once that are totally random and beyond our control. I bring that point up because at the exact moment my father's manhood was being challenged, a group of his friends, including my future mother, prowled the midway, drifting into his line of sight. The second and last nickel dropped into the carnie's hand. Again, my father fired a strike. Again, the same bottles fell and the same remained upright. Two more throws and he earned another whistle.

Broke and broken, he started to walk away when the group noticed his presence and waved, moving like a school of fish in his direction. He was a popular guy in school and what my children today might refer to as an *alpha male*.

"Them your friends?" asked the hustler.

"Yes."

"I like you. Ya got a good strong arm and ya seem like a nice kid."

"I'm glad *you* think so. My mom's going to kill me when I get home for losing her seed money."

"I can fix that problem and git you a little extra money, but you gotta do me one small favor."

"What?"

"Just throw these balls again like you did before."

"I told you, I'm out of money."

"I'll set you up for free. The only condition is whatever you win comes back to me after, except for one stuffed animal of yore choice, and I'll give you a quarter besides."

"A whole quarter?"

"Yep."

It seemed as if life had backed my father away from the abyss.

"And all I have to do is throw a baseball at those bottles again? What if I don't knock them down? I'm throwing my best right now."

"I think yore luck's gonna change. I'll risk it."

Juanita and the rest of his schoolmates, along with dad's older brother and a couple of his friends, arrived at the tent, shucking and jiving, laughing and squealing, innocent teenagers with full pockets of nickels and dimes saved from hours of paper routes, lawn mowings, house cleanings, and hay baling. Juanita laid her hand on John Bill's arm. "Are you going to win me a bear?" My father, who had just about decided not to throw again for fear of embarrassing himself if he still couldn't knock over the bottles, now had no choice. Her slightly aquiline nose, translucent, silk-like skin, and the husky sigh of her voice were more than a calloused farm boy could bear. He ran straight back to the edge of that void and leaped.

The rest of his friends crowded around as John Bill fired one true fastball after another. Milk bottles flew in all directions like coveys of frightened quail. His luck *had* changed. The black-toothed carnie spat, cursed, and then handed my father his choice of prizes. Finally, the carnie threw up his hands. "Stop it," he yelled over the laughter and excited buzzing of the crowd, which had increased exponentially with every clank of ball against bottle. "I can't afford to let you play no more," he said, gesturing at a huge stack of stuffed animals and costume jewelry on the counter. "Yore takin' all my profits."

Once John Bill stepped away from the counter, nickels and dimes rained down from all directions. Young men, old men, crazies, and cripples, grabbed for baseballs. The carnie, seeming confused and frightened, backed away from the counter and set the bottles on the stools again. "One at a time, one at a time. I can't keep up." But he did keep up and little by little all their money disappeared into his pocket. Not a single person, no matter how hard they tried, could duplicate my dad's success. Always…*always*, the two outside bottles on the bottom row remained upright.

Uncle Densil took his brother by the elbow, steering him away from the area and into the shadows behind the row of canvas tents, tripping over tent pegs and guide ropes. He took John Bill by the shoulders and shook him.

"Do you know what you're doing?"

"I'm earning enough money to get some extra seeds and this panda bear," said my father, shaking the fuzzy animal under my uncle's nose. "This bear might just convince Juanita that I'm a better catch than Peck."

"You're shilling for that carnie."

"I am not."

"You don't honestly believe you could knock all those bottles over so easily, do you?" asked Densil. "If it was that easy, the guy'd be out of business in ten minutes."

"Never thought about it. I *am* a pretty good pitcher, you know. Maybe my luck changed."

I believe that my father told the truth at this point. He wanted so badly to win a prize and undo the mistake of losing his mother's money that he never really considered the impossibility of his good fortune.

"Nobody's that good. Two of those bottles are loaded with lead weights. They wouldn't fall over if you hit them with a truck, unless those are the two you stack on top. The other three are made out of balsa wood. My job last summer was stacking bottles just like that for a different guy. Everybody's losing their money now based on what they saw you do. It's a shill game and you helped that asshole play it."

Realizing he was helping to cheat his friends, John Bill rushed back to the midway only to find the disappointed and empty-handed crowd dispersing out and my future mother going off to ride the Ferris wheel with Jim Peck. The carnival employee closed out the game by counting his money into a metal cash box.

"Come back for the money? Yore a pretty good shill. Couldn't interest you in comin' with us to the 4-H Fair in Albion, could I? Them boys over there is natural born suckers. We could clean 'em out the first day."

"You cheated my friends."

"No, *you* did. I just collected the money." He handed my father a shiny new quarter and said, "Here's yore share."

I suppose that my father might have refused the quarter, pummeled the greasy little man, or rounded up all of his buddies, or the sheriff, and retrieved the stolen money. He could have rushed over to my mother and presented her with his panda bear trophy right in front of Jim Peck. But, like many questionable situations he got himself into over the course of his life, John Bill simply took his earnings, hung his head in shame, and buried his guilt so deep in his subconscious that it remained innocuous unless it surfaced under the influence of too many martinis. The same was true of his male bravado. I don't mean bravery. My father came home from WWII a hero after serving three and half years in combat with the 82nd Airborne. I'm referring to that quality of the male ego that allows us a thick skin in intra-personal situations. He remained one of the most awkward men I ever knew around women he didn't know well and always felt out of place at social affairs and cocktail parties.

Much too humiliated to admit in front of any of his schoolmates that he had allowed himself, even unknowingly, to be manipulated into being an accomplice in the con game that relieved them of their hard-earned cash, he salved his conscience by purchasing extra seeds for my grandmother and won his repentance by working extra hours cultivating the family garden. From this experience, my dad formed a rule that he lived by all of his life, one I never realized myself until well beyond middle age – *never gamble with money you can't afford to lose.* He also developed a healthy skepticism for any deal that seemed too good to be true, along with an over-active obsession with honesty at all cost. I never saw or heard my father recommend any financial dealings for anyone without qualifying his advice by saying something like, "Be careful. A fool and his money are soon parted." Or, "This may not work out the way you expect." In that way, he never felt responsible for someone's reversal of fortune.

This was not an incident John Bill would have ever confessed to me. He had far too much pride to admit how easily he had been used. The tale would have been in poor taste and a bad example for his children. Nevertheless, Uncle Densil slipped up and shared the story one evening during the summer I returned home from Vietnam in 1969.

We sat on my grandmother's front porch drinking beer and watching the brightly colored people walk in and out of the brightly colored fairgrounds just across the road. I confessed my frustration and anger at being used by a government I trusted to fight an unjust war against a poor third world country for no apparent reason other than to line corporate pockets.

"You're not the first young man to find himself working as someone else's shill," he began as the barkers on the midway beckoned their prey.

While the stakes were exponentially higher in my war than in my father's con, the principle remains the same. We all use and get used. We all make choices in life that divide us into victim and villain simultaneously. The key to each choice lies in what lesson we bring away from the result. My father became an obsessively honest businessman from the moment he discovered the economic hardship to others and the emotional pain to himself of his dishonesty. Following his example, I've become a tireless and stentorian advocate of negotiation and non-violence since that moment in Quang Tri when I sighted another human being down the long blue-black barrel of my M-16 and with my sweaty cheek pressed tightly against the cold plastic stock gently squeezed the trigger.

Where Has All the Fancy Footwork Gone?

"Those move easiest who have learned to dance." – A. Pope

We are arriving at the past again. The economy and along with it the availability of meaningful employment in this 21st century seem to be traveling in a "back to the future" sort of direction. By that, I mean it is conceivable that the world may enter one day another economic catastrophe similar to the one my parents lived through in the 1930's. The causes may be slightly different, but the symptoms look the same. In the early 1930's thousands of jobs were being lost daily, people suffered and died from curable disease because health care was too expensive, food got rationed, lenders foreclosed on thousands of farms and homes, the environment became poison through bad farming and industrial practices, and the suicide rate climbed. A small group of wealthy elites controlled everything worth controlling. Interestingly, illegal immigrants flooded through the porous borders of western states taking what little migrant fruit-picking work existed; although, in an irony that only history can provide, the immigrants were American farmers from the Oklahoma dust bowl. When FDR was elected president and instituted social programs to help curb the catastrophic dissipation of our culture, he was labeled "socialist" by some and thought not radical enough by others. The truth of his reign rested somewhere in between. His programs provided the illusion of aid to the poor while benefiting bankers and corporate America the most.

World War II followed our last Great Depression and accomplished far more than FDR's paltry work programs in eliminating our economic woes. Oh sure, millions died. We dropped atomic bombs on unsuspecting civilians and decimated several great cultures, but our imperialistic capitalism thrived. I recognize the atrocities that made it necessary for humane reasons that America entered that war. But consider this. Nazis and the Japanese were committing those atrocities for years while we claimed neutrality. It was only after the Japanese attacked us at Pearl Harbor and endangered our strategic control of South Pacific shipping lanes that America declared herself actually in the fight on Japan first and Germany later. A strong case can be developed easily that, while we did a great humanitarian service for the world, our primary incentive was corporate. War is good business.

I, for one, am not sure that history must always repeat itself the way it continues to do. I believe that we can flourish as a nation and survive as a human race without resorting to an all-encompassing WWIII, even if we are dumb enough and callous enough to allow our politicians to keep killing off a few of our teenagers and slaughter thousands of third world peasants so corporate profits continue to roll in. How? Simple. We need to pay closer attention to the earliest of these pre-collapse symptoms, the way we dance. However improbable, it is possible that the way we dance may be a precursor of catastrophic events. If we learned to read correctly those indications in the future, we might well be on the road to foretelling and possibly preventing the repetition of a historical calamity brought about by another world war, sort of like a foot-stomping, music-emitting, Doppler radar.

Prior to the raising of my father's WWII generation, the Greatest one according to Tom Brokaw, there was communal dancing in every subculture and at every opportunity. From wedding to wake, any young rake who hoped to win a woman's heart needed to be able to step with her on the dance floor when the music started and both of them merge seamlessly into a community of graceful couples. My goodness, even Steinbeck in his incredibly brilliant and tragic novel *The Grapes of Wrath* has a long scene in which Tom Joad's family gets excited about a dance at a tent city full of starving Oakies because it creates a sense of shared hope and community.

Now it's true, dancing in those days meant a lot of different things just as it does today. You could have tripped the light fantastic, stomped a hoedown, slid a waltz, trotted with the fox, cake walked, or twirled elegantly with your partner in a European Redowa. If you happened to be an erudite urbanite immune to the economic blues, you might have found a club where you and a rather loose lady could Tango or shake the Maxixe. But whatever the tune, the purpose was always the same. Unlike walking, which has as its raison d'etre movement from point A to point B, dancing was designed to exorcise something intimate and offer it to a partner as your partner offered also to you something similar, a bond of humanity creating something greater than the sum of both your parts. In turn, the coupled harmony on the dance floor lifted whole groups of people together. Whether frustration, fear, anger, joy, hate, or love escaped, its release occurred through an act of shared grace that freed the dancers from their loneliest burdens.

I'm not trying to make a case that the Victorian generation invented dancing or that the forms of movement they created held any greater significance for them than for other tribes and cultures centuries before. Like the blues technique of call and response that originated in ancient sub-Saharan Africa rather than with B.B. King, dancing was one of man's earliest artistic achievements. Even King David was an avid dancer. My point here is to suggest that the type of intimate sharing with a partner that went on for centuries found its last adherents with the generation of my grandfather. As the 1920's roared in and my father's Depression-WWII generation grew, music and movement evolved into a wilder, more athletic exercise of self-flagellation, a way to exorcise the demons of excessive indulgence in personal pleasures. The Charleston, Black Bottom, Big Apple, Shag, and Jitterbug, shimmied and sweated their way into our collective psyche. This concern for the individual allowed the most ruthless and self-centered among society to capitalize on the devolving sense of community that degraded into economic chaos first and finally, a humanitarian nightmare. Oh yes, we fought our way out of that despair, but immediately began reliving the attitudes and social mores that put us in the wake of calamity just a few years earlier in our history.

Beginning with Baby-Boomers, Rock & Roll, and a new type of American philosophy evolving from sound bites such as McDonald's famous "you deserve a break today" and Burger King's "have it your way" and Budweiser's "this Bud's for you," the dancing paradigm made another huge leap, one that has helped alienate us from each other and provide the soil from which the black flowers of economic recession and war ultimately grow.

As my old man used to say every morning after promising my mother the night before he was going out for one drink only, "the road to hell is paved with good intentions." Our society's dance to hell all began righteously enough with the demise of the somnambulant Eisenhower decade of white, middle-class male prosperity. A counterculture of excessively bright and idealistic young people, brought into a world filled with racism, the threat of nuclear destruction, sexual repression, unjust wars, and gender inequality, evolved through the decade of the 1960's. Our intentions were to live as individuals according to the democratic ideals we had been taught in a public school system as children, principles formed from words like freedom, equality, justice, compassion, and honesty. We hoped to re-adjust our parents' attitudes toward these priorities that had been forsaken in pursuit of material security. Through individual attitudes and collect activism, the post-World War II Baby Boomer generation sought Utopia for every single citizen in the United States and peace throughout the earth.

Sounds great, right? The music and the dances generated by these good intentions helped to liberate us from the inhibitions our parents forced upon us as "civilizing" rules. We danced like tribal warriors and LBJ signed civil rights legislation into law. We danced and chanted like Buddhist bonzes and the draft ended, followed by the end of the Vietnam War. We pirouetted and grand-plied our way toward gender equality and control of our educational rights. All of this movement, including our dancing, was designed to achieve individual independence and through that a raising of humanitarian consciousness from which the entire society might benefit.

My old man used to always tell me, "No matter how thin you slice bread, it always has two sides." He was right literally and figuratively. Like bread when it is sliced, every social movement has two sides. The freer we became, the freer we wanted to be. We bopped, hopped, boogied, and skipped the Twist, the Mashed Potato, the Bristol Stomp, the Watusi, The Swim, Mickey's Monkey, and on the list goes with appendages flying in all directions, with every new step carrying us further away from each other and deeper inside ourselves. As external chains began falling away, we sought release from the internal ones that had bound us through drugs, among other things. Our dancing grew wilder and soon became a means of expanding self-expression without regard for dialogue. The most intimate form of human interaction, touch, was eliminated entirely. Shaking, twitching, shimmying, and writhing, the ecstasy soon progressed to goal rather than process and as it did, an attitude arose that the *only* requirement for utopia was this feeling of personal pleasure. We all deserved it. Our children should have it without earning it. Liberation of the soul was our gift to them as material prosperity had been our parents' gift to us. This was the illusion of social advancement and all the dancers in my generation bought into it.

We encouraged the generation after ours, commonly called Gen X, to build empires, multi-national corporations, stock portfolios, social welfare programs, and "open-enrollment" universities, all as a way to allow every individual the joy of immediate gratification with the threat of accountability so far into the distant future it lay somewhere beyond the vanishing point. Like dancing with a beautiful woman who happens to be some jealous guy's wife, it seemed as if the music would never end. Our banks handed out mortgages for mansions and Corvette Sting Rays. Children received credit cards before securing employment and soon refigured the axis of the earth so that it ran through each of them separately. As Gen X gave way to Gen Y and the New Millennials, people yearned to dance alone without regard for the "other" in any way, shape, or form. Like a marathon runner soon runs to beat his own best time rather than lead the pack, many life decisions are made in the

American middle-class and upward, in other words by the people who motivate and direct most aspects of this society, with regard to individual satisfaction alone. Responsibility is a cliché, a word always intended for someone else.

At this very moment, some young adult that you know may be doing The Carlton, The White Girl Overbite, The Bicycle Rack Dance, Hip Hop, or The Peacock with no other human visible for miles. Oh, there may be a pole for a partner, but little else. I'm not making a case that dancing alone is a bad thing. As with masturbation, everyone does it and it provides great relief. It can be fun. But most of us Baby Boomers discovered as we matured that something deeper, longer lasting, and more fulfilling requires sharing of the self. However, in the hope of sparing our children and grandchildren the emotional upheaval needed in learning that lesson, we never taught it to our children. We've encouraged new generations of young to believe every action taken must benefit the self first and foremost. By doing this, we've diminished the human race. The world has regressed to economic injustice and oligarchy. Petty wars fought to protect the financial interest of the oligarchs now threaten to erupt into a global conflagration at some point in the future. We find ourselves where we were almost a hundred years ago, dancing on the edge of a cliff with no one holding our hands.

As a teenager in the 1960's ready to embark on that quest for individualism and war and social activism, ready to explore the shadow places inside that drugs uncover, I ventured to the lower level in my father's new split-level ranch style home. I cranked up the stereo to the moans of Mick Jagger or the lamentations of Bob Dylan and flailed around in the darkness with the pretense of dancing for escape from adolescence and the reality of searching for a soul. The loneliness terrified and overjoyed me. The chaos overwhelmed me. Just when I thought that the room might explode, the doorbell rang. My uncle Jim was making his holiday visit.

I crept up the stairs as my father reached into a stack of old 78's and put one on his turntable in the living room, a Glenn Miller song.

Uncle Jim took my mother's hand, and they glided over the hardwood floor in their socks with a rustling sound. My father was an adequate dancer, and he loved his wife, but he knew that my uncle *loved* to dance and was spectacular on the floor. And he knew my uncle was lonely. Dad's act may seem a small gesture, relatively meaningless in the grand scheme of things. Still, watching the elegance and grace of these two moving together like Fred Astaire and Ginger Rogers made us all smile and feel a little better. That's precisely what I miss in this new world, the world that's beginning to resemble the old one.

Crazy

In April of 1969, The United States Marine Corps gave me an honorable discharge. I had come back home from Vietnam slightly off time with the rest of the world like a cheap pocket watch wound too tight. Bruised and battered physically and emotionally, as were many of my fellow veterans, I returned to the college classes I deserted in 1966 when I enlisted. My life went forward, but with little, or no, enthusiasm for academics. Over the next year and a half, I took up campus politics and got myself elected president of the student senate just to see if I could, developed a wicked addiction to amphetamines and briefly married another speed-freak. Our speed-induced paranoia and Christianized guilt combined with the harping of both her parents and mine had tied our stomachs in tight knots and cut off blood flow to what was left of the sensible parts of our brains. In response to these dark emotions created by God, we had a small service at a church in Haubstadt, Indiana. My friend Spyder O'Neil served as the best man and then we spent our honeymoon drinking Cold Duck and smoking black hash in the back seat of my car.

By late winter of 1970 or early spring in 1971, I'm not sure anymore, a vague, but constant uneasiness crept into my mind. Part of this existential dread had to do with the fact that we ran out of good speed two days before. Our regular dealer, a guy named Joe who always gave us pharmaceutical quality dope, had yet to receive his new supply from his mother (a whole other story). I was strung-out, fried to the max. But another feeling pulled at me as well, as if I swam in one of the deceptive rivers close by. I glided along with a soft and smooth current that ran quietly on the surface but often found myself exhausted because of fighting a swift undertow that had been present since my marriage. I struggled for the chance to keep myself afloat against what I now recognize as a persistent state created by the absence of war in my psyche. It was boredom. Maybe it wasn't so much boredom as a feeling of urgency because I had come to understand how fragile life could be. I had somewhere, although I had no idea where, to get to and my present situation held me back.

After snorting a line of crystal meth before classes one morning, I began crashing by the time I got home in the late afternoon. This was the day Todd, who later became a lawyer in New Orleans, showed up with several of our "friends" at the apartment door with his super-duper red acid tablets.

While arguing with my wife about some inconsequential matter, the acid kicked in. The first few hours of bright colors, reverberating sounds, and animated traces of movement in the air caused laughter all around the room. I reveled in the feeling of oneness with my companions, as if I were inside them and part of them. My love for Becky brought me to tears. I frolicked with the gods and melted into the stars that I thought were visible through my roof. Somewhere in the middle of me returning to stardust the acid began to peak and grate against the cheap meth paranoia. The trip went sideways.

The wall in the living room collapsed and on the other side, instead of my bedroom, Vietnam beckoned. The hallucination swallowed me in a suffocating quicksand of terror. Body parts covered the floor. Tracer rounds shot by my head. I ducked, bounced, hid behind the couch. The smell of cordite and gunpowder filled the air. Men screamed. The top of Todd's head blew off. My wife morphed into an old Vietnamese woman and when she tried to comfort me, her features distorted into dozens of Russell's vipers. Covering my head with my hands, I screamed – Incoming – and couldn't stop. Incoming… Incoming… Incoming…

Obviously, screams were an unwanted distraction in an apartment building where the walls were made of sheetrock as thin as skin on the forehead. I became unmanageable rapidly. In their desire to keep the police away from the door, Todd, my wife, and my other friends fed me several Seconal capsules. Being a powerful barbiturate, the Seconal quieted me, and I was escorted to my bed where I writhed and sweated for hours as the chemicals in my bloodstream fought each other for control of my mind. I could have died, but all I did finally was fall into a peaceful sleep. The dreams contained no people or concrete images, only crystalline pieces of bright colors, as if someone turned a kaleidoscope in my brain.

Twenty hours of time evolved into twilight of the next day, and I woke up in my bed alone. Dusky, grey light filtered in through the windows, limbo light, some purgatory between life and death, sanity and madness, peace and war. I walked from my bed to the mirror, gazing with wonder at the apparition. My skin gave off a grey glow like the light in the room. For the longest time, I couldn't tell which image was real, the one in the mirror or the one staring at it.

Panic, deeper than anything experienced in combat, leaked up through my subconscious and seeped into my consciousness like dirty oil. There were no more excuses like combat trauma and shell shock I had made to myself in the hospital in Japan when I hallucinated the faces of dead comrades after being wounded in Vietnam. However, once again as at that time, I accepted the unthinkable possibility that I had gone crazy, uselessly, hopelessly out of my mind.

The next several weeks drowned me in a sea of insanity. I drank eight glasses of water a day because I read somewhere they prevented acid flashes. I paced the floor at night locking and relocking the apartment door. Faces distorted when I blinked my eyes as if made from Play Dough, and I guarded my food religiously, afraid it was poisoned. By spring break I quit attending classes, no longer able to look my wife in the face without seeing those snakes. I refused to touch or swallow anything that looked like a pill out of sheer terror, which confused Becky and caused her to take more drugs. Our arguments roared on constantly and always about nothing.

To her credit, she didn't give up on our relationship right away and scheduled an appointment with a local psychiatrist for marriage counseling. We made one visit. Becky confessed that my irrational harangues created ideas of suicide in her, for which this particular doctor promptly prescribed massive doses of life-threatening barbiturates.

Thinking it might save us both, I moved out of the apartment and into an old farmhouse with four people I barely knew who had no connections with my speed dealer, Joe. When my wife called me one last time, it was to ask that I set up another appointment with the psychiatrist. Agreeing, I talked with his office assistant and discovered that the doctor had recently become despondent. He walked out on his front porch, threw a rope over a rafter, and hung himself late one night, causing acute psychological trauma for the paperboy the following dawn.

The idea that the man trying to save us couldn't save himself did little to bolster my confidence in therapy, or even in the idea that answers to our problems existed. I withdrew further and spent long hours alone in my room reading a new novel written by William Peter Blatty. The novel was entitled The Exorcist, and by the middle of the book I began to feel possessed by Satan. Voices hung in the shadows. Walls breathed in and out. A heavy weight lay on my chest every time I lay down to sleep. In the sleepless moonlit room, red spots danced around like flaming fireflies. I rose every few minutes to make sure the doors were locked. It did no good. The danger had burrowed deep within my own body and mind.

I fought these symptoms of paranoid schizophrenia alone, not realizing at the time that they were chemically induced. I was afraid that by discussing them with another person, my secret dementia would become public, and I would be locked away somewhere forever. The delusional quality of my fears became apparent to me in a few months. However, in the initial phase of my self-induced de-tox, they were all very real.

Adding to my anxiety, Becky and I agreed to divorce, and in April of 1971, the process was put in motion by her lawyer. We had no children and almost no property. Consequently, the matter was handled legally without my presence over a period of the next few months. But, to me, all the paperwork was nothing more than formality. My marriage had seemed like a vague dream since the moment I quit using drugs.

During this period, I lost myself completely and fought for familiar and tangible touchstones to hold onto much like a drowning man gropes for a life preserver. I went to mass every day even though not a practicing Catholic. Some comfort came to me from the repetitive rituals, but I stopped attending when the icons in the church rectory kept distorting into delusional demons flying at me while parishioners made their collective confession of faith. Even Jesus bled from his cross high above the altar, often shaking his fist at me as the priest chanted undecipherable Latin phrases.

All I could remember from my high school Latin classes revolved around the phrase "dead language" and that made me panic further. I tried pronouncing the words backwards, like playing an album backwards on the turntable, hoping to find some secret message left by God in the masking.

Finally, the week before final exams I returned to Southside Bar & Grill for an afternoon of drinking draft beer and shooting pool. The bar still served as an old hangout for the fraternity I had pledged during my first year of college before the war and the drugs. I guess that I secretly hoped to run into a few of my frat brothers. Since I'd met Becky, I hadn't seen much of them, and they must have not noticed I had gone missing because none of them had tried to contact me, except for Marty Frazier, who begged me for a two-dollar loan.

Marty had choked himself on the morning I bumped into him. He invoked his morning ablutions as usual, draining several half empty beer cans left on various tables from the poker games in the frat house the night before. However, on this morning, Marty swallowed a couple of soggy Marlboro butts extinguished in the last can. He needed a fresh six-pack of beer to wash the foul taste away, and I happened to be the first familiar face he saw that might have the money. So much for brotherhood.

Southside unfolded into a narrow rectangle about the size of two parallel train cars. Sawdust sifted between my toes and the soles of my sandals as I worked my way toward the bar. On my left, two young men with high and tight haircuts and bulging biceps played a lethargic game of pool, probably military personnel on leave. They stopped talking to stare at my disheveled clothes and shoulder length hair, not so much in anger as envy, and then returned to chalking their cue sticks.

Against the wall on my right a couple played bar shuffleboard. The girl leaned across the end of the long sand-covered wood surface, and the way she stroked the puck back and forth in the grit with her hand, slowly and deliberately, before letting it slide down the runway excited me with an animal lust I hadn't felt since becoming one of the flower children. Her breast grazed the veneered surface as she let go. When she stood straight up, her nipples were hard, a few grains of sand strategically encircling them. She squealed and bounced up and down as the puck glided to a stop on one of the numbers. The boyfriend, a red-faced and dumpy farmer, caught me staring and smiled as if to say—*I get this whenever I want and you don't*—and then patted her ass. Embarrassed that he could read my mind, I turned my head quickly toward the bar.

The bartender Phil was a middle-aged reprobate with hair the color and viscosity of used motor oil, a face full of pock marks, and eyes hard and narrow as slivers of coal. I recognized him from the many nights of rowdy beer drinking in my past and, like a good diplomat of drunkenness, he remembered me.

"What the hell happened to you, boy? D'ya forget where the barber set up shop?"

"Just a change in attitude, Phil. Give me a drink."

"You ain't a commie now, are ya. 'Cause I'm a veteran. You see that flag?"

He pointed to a huge confederate flag nailed above the wide mirror and below a neon Pabst Blue Ribbon sign.

"No commie. Just thirsty. I'm a veteran too."

"What'll it be."

I looked at the long row of cheap bar whiskey, gin, and vodka on the shelf behind him and then at my reflection in the mirror, struggling for a moment to recognize the person I saw. I wasn't sure if the sallow cheeks in the mirror belonged to the person on the bar stool, or if the image watched the reality. My stomach churned. My bowels loosened as if they would void soon in my pants. When the wave of paranoia subsided, I pointed to the Budweiser tap.

"One of those, I guess."

Taking the beer to one of the many empty tables, I pulled back a chair, sat and propped my feet up in the chair next to me. The beer was cold and tasted good. I began to remember a life of baseball diamonds and blonde cheerleaders named Katie that lived in a fantasy time of ancient history. I drank two more and felt my body relax. I may have even dozed a bit, my face warmed by the sunlight streaming in the windows. Just when I felt most comfortable my father walked through the door. At first he appeared as a broad shadow with the sun at his back through the screen. Questioning the reality of this apparition, I came to attention in my chair and began looking for an escape route.

As soon as his voice echoed through the bar, I knew his body was real and then, freezing me in rigid position, the fear came. His presence, the fact that he had taken time away from habitual routine and had driven all the way here to find me, was so out of character that I could imagine only the most horrible of reasons. My mother must have died, my sister Sandy must have gotten married, or the automobile business must have gone belly up.

"How'd you know where I was?"

"I stopped by that house of idiots you call fraternity brothers, and some guy named Marty said I might catch you here."

My father seemed much older than his half a century. His once broad and straight shoulders rolled into a tired slump as he sat next to me. The crooked nose had swollen and turned red from too many years of drinking Beefeater's gin. Deep lines road mapped the formerly smooth forehead and trailed off around anxious brown eyes. He wasn't drunk, but smelled of drinking. The suntan he proudly wore the year around was a faded, jaundiced shade of rusty yellow. Beneath the sad expression, I could feel anger seething.

"I got bored studying and thought a beer might help."

"You look like shit."

"Thanks."

"Your mother wants to kill herself."

"What are you talking about?"

"You heard me. Your mother wants to kill herself. I had to sell my guns and hide the valium. This is all your fault."

"You drove down here from Princeton, Indiana, to blame me because you think mom wants to kill herself? Philosophically speaking, that's a personal choice."

Realizing now how tenuous the hold is on sanity in this culture of ours to begin with, how much most of us struggle daily to find reason for going on, I can barely imagine myself spitting out those cruel, stupid, and useless words. In my father's place, I might have broken my son's jaw for making a remark like that.

He rolled his eyes and squeezed his broad hands into fists, and then jumped up. Walking to the bar, he leaned over and spoke in Phil's ear. The bartender nodded and poured him a glass of gin over ice.

"I drove down here to tell you we can't take it anymore. All this hippie crap and long hair. We know you're smoking pot. We can't keep giving you money to live like this. Your mother thinks she's failed as a parent. She can't sleep. She barely eats any more. She's hot one minute and freezing the next. She talks crazy half the time, wants me to give up playing cards and can't stand to be left alone. She hasn't had a period in months. Hell, I was used to fighting with her a week every month. Now, she nags me twenty-four hours a day every day. And, it's always about little shit that doesn't matter, the trash, doing dishes, cleaning the gutters, how it's no good cooking for just the two of us anymore. The doctor says it's a normal occurrence at her age when everything stops working, but the real reason is she's worried to death about you. I know it is. You've got to do something about it."

"I'm doing fine. Tell her not to worry."

"No. You come home and tell her not to worry. Cut your hair, gain some weight. Straighten out that thing you call a marriage."

The air in Southside stopped moving. My father drained his glass of gin. For the first time, I noticed the slight nervous tic above my left eye that stayed with me for two years. I tried to make it stop, but as I concentrated on control, the tic got worse. Confusion seeped, like hot candle wax, into my once clear thoughts and burned them with sorrow. Was I really the bad person with no sense of gratitude that my father described, or a visionary who saw the world changing into something my parents couldn't understand? It was true, they sent me money every month to supplement the G.I. Bill, but didn't they owe me that for bringing me into the world. The ambivalence brought me to the edge of screaming.

He spoke for several more minutes, keeping his head lowered and staring at the cocktail napkin on the table top, reminding me of all the material goodness, including cars and clothes, he and my mother had lavished on me as I grew up, how they struggled to give me the best home life possible, how he had lived during the Great Depression, wore his brother's hand-me-downs, worked as a shill at the county fair one year just to buy seeds for the family garden, how he never complained when I quit playing basketball in high school or lost my baseball scholarship to Kentucky Wesleyan, and how there comes a time in every man's life when he has to grow up, actually become a man. Everything he said was accurate. I didn't want to know it, but I did know it

This was no dialogue; this was another one of the very familiar lectures my father gave me on my duties as a male in American society. It enraged me that my service in Vietnam seemed to mean nothing to him. What I didn't understand at the time was his inability to deal with the way the war affected me. He spent three and a half years as a paratrooper during WWII, making combat jumps into several European battles. Then Dad came home to a local tickertape parade, married his high school sweetheart, and began a successful business. Life went on. I think he assumed that should be the case with his son as well. But, like most Viet vets who spent time in the bush hunting for Victor Charley and came home as a social pariah, it wasn't.

When he finished the litany of labors, he warned me that, unless I returned home after finals with a haircut, clean clothes, and diploma in hand, no more money would be forthcoming from the family coffer. Then, he stood, shook my hand firmly, and disappeared.

The whole episode felt bizarre, a surreal dream of my life within the surreal dream of my life. I had no idea how to process and use the information received. The idea that menopause, both male and female, had invaded the McGarrah family never occurred to me at the time. Even though its existence had been around for as long men reached a *middle age* and women reached the end of ovulation, doctors and psychologists had only recently discovered ways to define this fraying of mind and body around the edges of oncoming old age.

For a few minutes, I accepted willingly some responsibility for my mother's aberrant behavior and my father's frightening anxiety, but I wasn't good with responsibility in those days. So, I drank two more beers and drove back to the place where I stayed and did the only thing I knew how to do in the limbo days, those days between form and substance, shadow and light, those times when living had become an illusion and the struggle to exist, my only reality. I slept like a baby.

This confession of my self-centered, horrible behavior wasn't written to excuse that behavior. I have come to accept the fact that I was not a good person after I came home from Vietnam. I was no hero, just a dumb American somewhere between victim and villain. But years later after much therapy, I learned to understand that my experiences in combat had caused a break in my mind, an actual physical injury to my brain like the wounds received to my body, known as Post Traumatic Stress disorder. Hell, the Veterans Administration didn't even recognize it as an injury, a moral one, existed until fourteen years after my return.

What I have attempted to do by relating it is to remind all of us that thousands of men and women who, if they're lucky, and come home from these little police actions and limited wars our government keeps using to protect American political and business interests in the 21st century are new generations given wounds that may not be obvious or even noticeable physically. But they do exist. People return from the obscenity of combat broken. If not in body, almost always in mind. We, as a society, have a moral and ethical responsibility to recognize it and help them recover just as much as they have a responsibility to face this reality and struggle through it, if they can. We all suffer if we don't accept that responsibility.

How We Have All Become Prisoners

I came home from Vietnam, left the Marine Corps in 1969, and returned to college. I had flunked out of said college a few years before and lost a baseball scholarship through the over-enjoyment of fraternity keg parties. My time in a war led me to re-evaluate what my father meant by his admonition that "fools learn through experience what wise men learn by being told," and I decided that a return to education from books would be healthier than to one by bullets.

During one summer break in the early 1970's, my close friend Spyder O'Neil and I traveled from campus to his home town of Chester, New York where we spent the summer working as maintenance men at a bungalow colony on the edge of the Catskill Mountains. The whole area was heavily populated with these properties spotted with small cabins that were full of Manhattan families every summer in those days. If you've seen *Dirty Dancing*, you get the idea of setting and place but without the Hollywood romantic nonsense.

The pay was decent, and the work less than challenging, luckily because we didn't know the difference between pliers and saws. More importantly, the state of New York was experimenting with a lowered drinking age of eighteen at that time. Consequently, we drove to nearby Middletown two or three nights a week full of energy and sporting a pocket full of cash. On most Middletown nights, the streets were full of young women home from college themselves, and Spyder and I were filled with the hope of picking up any number of beautiful coeds. Although this hope was dashed on a regular basis, we never gave up.

One particular night, we ducked into a small bar somewhere off the main drag for a quick shot of whiskey and a glass of draft beer. The cave-like room was dark, dimly lit, and nearly empty. Sawdust and litter scattered around our sneakers as we walked over to some stools and climbed on them. The bartender brought over two Schafer drafts in frosted mugs, and since I had declared myself on a psychedelic sabbatical, Spyder dropped a hit of mescaline into his alone. After twenty minutes and another beer, he began to ride a solitary rainbow composed of traces from the neon lights above the mirror that hung over the shelf of bottles behind the bar. I smiled as I watched him breaking pretend bubbles of various colors, jabbing them with a finger and giggling like a two-year-old.

A new customer entered. He took a seat on a stool two empty ones away from me. Taciturn and with a left eye that twitched every few seconds, the man appeared to be around fifty years old. His dark hair was neatly trimmed, graying around his ears, and swept back into what we used to call a duck tail that passed out of popularity after James Dean managed to kill himself in a car wreck. The skin on his face was worn leather, deeply tanned and well scuffed with wrinkles. The nose spread a little too wide and flat and crooked at the bridge, a sure sign it had been broken before. The jeans were new, and his shirt stiffly starched and buttoned all the way up his neck to the collar. Even in the neon glow of the bar light, I could detect a yellowish tint in his eyes. All in all, he seemed to be lost. Every minute or so he glanced over his right shoulder to check the door as if waiting for something or someone.

After sipping about half of a Budweiser in a bottle, he turned toward me and offered an opinion. This wasn't that unusual in those days. There were no strangers in a place like a tavern.

"Cars look a lot different now than they did fifteen years ago." I nodded. But he said nothing else while he drink another beer. Finally, he turned to face me on his stool and asked if I knew of any restaurants nearby that were cheap and made a good cheeseburger. I was struck by how gently he spoke and how sad his eyes looked, almost like an old dog in a kennel that had accepted the fact it would never be rescued.

"There's a McDonald's if you walk to the stoplight on the corner, turn left and walk a block. You'll see the big yellow arches." I answered and smiled. "I can't guarantee you'll get a great cheeseburger, but it will be cheap."

"McDonald's? What kind of food do they serve? Is it a fancy place?"

"It's a McDonald's, my man. They got the same menu from New York to California, and all stops in between."

"That don't tell me nothing. I've never been in one."

"No?"

"They didn't exist fifteen years ago. Almost nothing is like it was."

"Fifteen years? You been out of the country in the Army? I spent some time overseas myself."

"Not exactly. I been in prison."

That's where the conversation ended. I was curious, but sometimes you don't press a man for information. If it's personal and he wants, he'll explain. If not, it's what we used to say in grade school. It's a nunya, none of your fucking business. This seemed like one of those occasions. For a long time, my perspective on this was uncomplicated, and I've written about that before. I used to believe freedom was being able to do what we wanted that was safe and comfortable without being challenged too much and without hurting other people. When we can't do those things that we are used to doing or expect to be able to do, no matter how trivial, especially those everyday things we take for granted, things get confused, disconnected, out of balance. We've lost our freedom. What gave me a new perspective was the fact that the man in the bar left shortly and tried to break into a jewelry store. Soon arrested, they sent him back to prison for violating his parole. The story in the newspaper that I read about that incident quoted him as saying that "he felt freer in prison and wanted to go back."

After living in America for the last fifty years since this incident, I believe now that I got things wrong. What many of us "white folk" in

America—and I'm basing this on what I read, conversations with the public, and comments on social media—is a freedom from change. We want to never be uncomfortable with our thoughts, our beliefs, our environment, or our opinions. We want an invisible caste in which we are dominant and controlling. Our white male masters in power understand the only way to give us this feeling that is to isolate ourselves from "the other" diverse peoples we should be welcoming into this country. We are locked in our own cages built out of fear that a changing demographic and an open environment that welcomes other cultures, traditions, and ideas will destroy the status quo, ironically the very thing that keeps us from the freedom our Constitution is supposed to provide.

Thankfully, not all of us feel this way because there has never been a time in history that I know of when isolation has proven to be conducive to constructive growth for a society. No single race of humans that I know can fulfill all the needs of an increasingly diverse society by refusing to accept change, by fearing the contributions and ideas from sources other than the status quo. The failure of Colonialism and slavery in the 19th century and the horror of the 3rd Reich in the 20th proved this, at least to some of us. We are at a stage when we can choose stagnation and the limitations that come from walling ourselves off from the influences of other races and other attitudes. But, consider the fact that the recidivist rate in the United States prison system is over 70%. If isolation or control of power and policy by a single race is the key to making better citizens, and fear of change the key to emotional and spiritual growth then why is more than two-thirds of our criminal population incapable of progressing to a better life when the opportunity presents itself?

I don't know. Maybe this is a stupid analogy for our great thinkers and leaders. I am neither a great thinker nor a leader. But when I see the Supreme Court overturning progressive laws like the right for women to control their own bodies, when I see South American children drowning because of a river strung with barbed wire, factual history deleted from high school textbooks, LGBT citizens treated with hatred, transgender teenagers denied health care, politicians refusing climate change, or the worship of a demagogic con man as a raison d'etre for our country, it seems like the direction we might be headed. And I am not convinced it's the right one.

The Gods Are Not Accountable

"Everywhere man blames nature and fate, yet his fate is mostly but the echo of his character and passions, his mistakes and weaknesses."

– Democritus.

In a time of tragedy, it is customary to speak polite phrases, to utter soft words of comfort, to offer a pint of Ben & Jerry's "Chocolate Therapy" instead of saying what needs to be said even if it tastes like a mouthful of "Ass in the Tub of Armageddon Special Reserve Hot Sauce." There have been more than 250 major incidents in schools alone since Columbine, not counting malls, churches, movie theaters, strip clubs, hospital emergency rooms, and urban street corners. A major incident is classified as a shooting in which two or more people are injured or killed. There have been more than sixty mass murder events since 1982 involving firearms and almost a third of those have happened within the last few years. So, unfortunately for you, dear readers, my thoughts in the aftermath of the latest mass murder will drive my language more toward peppery heat than sweet ice cream.

Raise your eyes and read the epigraph above my words again, carefully. Democritus wrote this long before anyone thought of gunpowder, much less rifles that fire thirty rounds in less than fifteen seconds even if it doesn't have a selector switch and is a *semi*-automatic. Every time some maniac decides to go off on a room full of people to get attention, we offer up platitudes to the families of the victims and logical fallacies to ourselves to salve our own consciences without ever addressing the real issue. Somewhere, deep down inside, those of us that have any humanity left understand exactly what this ancient Greek meant. These horrible acts continue and multiply exponentially every few years, not because fate has decreed that certain people should die at a certain time or because nature requires the sacrifice of innocent children. No, these events have become an "echo of our character" as a nation.

Of the firearms used in all mass shootings since 1982, 75% were purchased legally. What happens to the argument that I hear frequently from the semi-literate fools who have managed to co-opt the once respectable and viable organization that used to be the NRA – "We don't need more laws to control our guns. Pretty soon the government will take all our guns away." Is this the only truth we should consider even if it was possible?

First, let's look at the language people with actual sense are using. Control and eliminate are not synonyms. I own several guns, and I have never heard anyone threaten to take them away. I have never seen any major movement to ratify the Constitution with a new amendment that renders the second one moot. Even if someone in Congress brought it up, even if someone passed a bill and sent it out to the states, do you really believe there are enough voters to provide 38 states with the majority votes necessary to change the 2nd Amendment? If you do, I have a bridge in Brooklyn that I'll sell you – cheap.

How about this argument? "We got background checks so criminals and crazies can't buy no weapons." Check this fact out, people. Some 40% of the legally owned guns in this country get sold on the internet and at traveling gun shows. Guess what you don't have to pass to buy a gun from these venues. Yep, you guessed correctly, a background check. Let me translate that for you. Four out of every ten legally sold firearms may have been sold to felons or psychos, and if so, we wouldn't know it.

Do you think I'm finished with my little rant? Not hardly. Here's a sterling piece of logic I always enjoy hearing. "If everybody had a gun these things wouldn't happen." I heard it after Aurora, Colorado, as they carted the bodies away from the movie theater. Having engaged in several night fire fights at close range with high powered assault rifles handled by expertly trained users, I thought to myself – Brilliant! Wouldn't it have been fantastic for dozens of untrained and terrified people to be firing weapons in a darkened theater? One of our esteemed congressmen, the gentleman from Texas (where else?), the right honorable Louie Gomert stated that if only the principal at Sandy Hook was gifted with her own assault rifle she could have "taken the shooter's head off." This genius who helps run our government managed to spit these words out while the blood of babies was still warm on classroom floors, and they are repeated ad nauseum after every slaughter. Never mind the training and mental discipline required to walk at someone firing a weapon and fire back with enough accuracy to hit a target. Never mind the fact that this whole event ended in two minutes, barely time for the principal to unlock a drawer, remove a rifle, load a magazine, and chamber a round. Maybe Republicans expect our teachers to patrol classrooms locked and loaded, selectors set on full auto.

Two of the most ridiculous bumper stickers printed—"If we outlaw guns, only outlaws will have guns" and "Guns don't kill people, people do"—adorn thousands of vehicles from rusted-out Chevy pickup trucks to Lincoln Navigators. Back to my first point, no one in political power has EVER *seriously* discussed outlawing all guns. I would like the NRA to stop using that as an excuse to try and make tanks and missiles available to the public. For the other half of that phrase, how many outlaws do you know that go around shooting people indiscriminately. To a criminal, a gun is one of the tools he or she uses to accomplish a crime. Felons keep a low profile to avoid arrest. They don't engage in mass shootings, public displays of brandishing guns, or target random individuals for hate crimes and to make social statements. Maybe they will have guns, but they won't be the only ones. So will the police, and the police will be targeting them for committing specific crimes.

As for the other astute statement, we all know that people kill people with things other than guns. For example, in England where it is extremely difficult to obtain a firearm permit and almost no one owns a handgun there were 564 homicides in 2011, around 60 of those were caused by bullets. During the same period in the U. S. almost 11,000 men, women, and children managed to lose their lives by gunfire. So yeah, people do kill people. They just do it a whole hell of a lot less frequently when they have to work at it rather than simply pull the trigger of a rifle feed by a drum magazine.

I'm not against having a gun in the home. I keep one loaded in a drawer in my bedroom and another one in my office. But I used to make my living with a gun, and I taught pistol marksmanship in the Marine Corps. I'm aware of how to use the pistols I own, and I respect them. I understand as well that guns in the home will account for 22 times more injuries and death by suicide, by accident, and by family argument rather than through self-defense. This proves to me that a lot of people with guns for protection are not really protected, especially from themselves. Being honest I will tell you that being used to and careful with guns does not always preclude stupidity. I had a negligent discharge from a 9mm semi-auto pistol once while I was cleaning it and blew a hole through a piece of my wife's antique furniture. To this day, I still don't know where that round in the chamber came from. My son was sitting next to me at the time, and my carelessness terrifies me when I remember it. Bad shit happens, but there's usually a stupid reason for it.

If I seem angry here, it's because I am. I'm very angry with myself and you, the American public. I feel guilty about Columbine, Sandy Hook, Aurora, Tucson, and on and on and on and on. These horrible tragedies are my fault and yours, not because we pulled the triggers, not because we have "personality" disorders, but rather because we are apathetic and cowardly. We have allowed ourselves to be bullied and used by corporations that make billions of dollars selling assault style rifles and drum magazines to anyone with enough money to buy them. Rather than research the problem for ourselves, we have allowed propaganda voices in the media like Fox News to create an atmosphere of hate and paranoia that the crazies take for a call to arms. It's easier to believe what people say than to actually think about it.

We all sat on our asses and did nothing while greedy politicians closed state run hospitals during the Reagan administration and forced thousands of mentally ill people to be housed in prisons, prisons run by private corporations that needed the head count to keep profits up. Does it seem reasonable that human beings suffering from delusions, hallucinations, and a host of other debilitating disorders will get better by having violent sociopaths for neighbors? Each one of these disturbed people will be given medicine with very little treatment or true help and, at some point when they appear halfway functional, be released back into mainstream society. Maybe you will be standing next to one at a gun show where both of you can legally purchase a Bushmaster rifle without a background check.

I don't want things to be this way anymore. At my age, I live in the presence of death every day. It's the paradox of human life. We share the joy of living with the knowledge that one day we will grow old and die. We learn to balance that joy and anguish in our later years so that we are not paralyzed with fear daily. We accept our passing as part of nature. But the human mind doesn't really begin to face mortality until we are somewhere past middle age. That's for our own protection, for our sanity. I don't want our children to live in the presence of death before puberty. I don't want them anxious over issues of mortality. I don't want them terrified to go to school or the movies. It isn't a fair trade-off just so I can sit legally in my recliner with a six pack of beer and stroke my AK-47 as I watch old Rambo films. I'm tired and ashamed of my own compliance. I'm going to scream, bitch, moan, irritate, aggravate, and vote until somebody listens, until we get better gun *control*, until we get adequate health care for the mentally ill, until our society re-evaluates its priorities, and until we get back to compassion as the driving force of democracy. We don't need a lot of new, more severe, gun restrictions. We need to exercise common sense and balance in implementing the ones we have, and maybe tweak some of them so they work better. After all, it's our responsibility as citizens. Like Democritus, I can no longer blame nature and fate when my own passions, mistakes, and weaknesses are controlling my destiny.

A Remembrance of Weeds

I'm seventy-six years old standing under a bright, white sun in a battered straw hat holding a tool I have not held in my hands for sixty years called a sickle. It is 97 degrees Fahrenheit in July in central Georgia. The borders around my lawn surround me with an army composed of Oxtail, Lespedeza, Nutsedge, Bittercress, and Wild Onions, among other rapscallions enlisted by an enemy government called Weeds. The battle will soon begin, reluctantly on my part because I know it's a war that cannot be won. Nevertheless, my wife has drafted me into this fight with no regard for the sacrifice required by my body, broken and bent by decades of misuse and abuse from the pleasures of living with what she calls vices. Such is the struggle of retirement. Without a job, I can no longer rely on the plaintive cry of "I've got work to do and don't have time, Dear."

Before the initial engagement and through the heat, sweat, and anxiety of worry about heatstroke, and heart attack, a memory sneaks into my consciousness. I'm in high school, trying to keep gasoline in the tank of my beautiful '57 Chevy Belair. Even though fuel for cruising a circle around two drive-in soda shops—one Called Dick Clark's and the other called Winkler's—always populated in the humid evenings by the loveliest car hops and classmates in my hometown cost a mere twenty cents a gallon, that price was above my insignificant amount of earning power. The struggle for cash was constant.

My father owned an automobile dealership that could be called successful by economic standards in the 1960's. However, part of his success relied on the belief that money should be earned, not given. Consequently, I was forced by circumstance to beg him for some summer employment that would augment the pitiful allowance he afforded me based on something he called principles. He agreed to my begging with a satirical smile. My dad knew the thing I most despised as a teenager was lawn work. It interfered with American Legion baseball, stealing beer off the neighbor's back porch, and swimming most days in the old coal-mining strip pits that had been reclaimed and that dotted Gibson County, Indiana. Consequently, and with devilish glee I believe, my first task was to trim weeds from the borders of his office building. He handed me a long wooden stick with a curved metal blade.

"This is called a sickle. It's the best tool for removing unwanted weeds."

"How does it work?"

"Swing it like you do your Louisville Slugger, son. It doesn't take a genius to figure it out. It belonged to your grandmother, and she taught me and your Uncle Ding to use it well when we were much younger than you."

I looked skeptical. There was no motor like the one on our new power lawn mower from Sears & Roebuck bought recently to help eliminate violent arguments when I was forced to cut our lawn at home once a week. Also, when I surveyed the assigned area, it grew to the size of the football field at Lowell school in my mind, a place of torture where I would soon begin bruising my body with autumn practice.

We argued. I reminded him that Indiana had several laws forbidding child labor. He responded.

"You haven't been a child since your first nocturnal emission."

"I'm still the smallest guy in my class, except for you know who." You Know Who being a friend and very nice fellow who had lost a testicle early in life by falling on the cross bar of his bicycle. At least he had an excuse for being small. All I had was a chip on my shoulder the size of a boulder, but that's another story entirely.

"Whatever you do watch out for wiring on the new air conditioning unit and anything else that could possibly be damaged. You could tear up a blacksmith's anvil."

My father felt especially proud of the air conditioning. In those days, sweltering summer heat and humidity did not guarantee that every home and every business would be an oasis of cool comfort. It was still an expensive appliance and in its relative infancy.

So, it began. The travail of a teenaged Don Quixote. I looked at the green growing from the foundation around his bright, whitewashed stone building. The north side stretched some twenty-five yards along the gravel on the Main Street lot to an intersection where it turned east for fifteen yards to the other corner and then back along Prince Street to the other corner creating a rectangle of agony of sweat and monotony. My tee-shirt was soaked before I ever took the first swing. Anyone who has survived the ninety-plus degrees of "dog days" in Southern Indiana will relate to the external steam room I'm describing.

In a fit of rage and hatred for all things green, I tore along the building with sparks jumping from the sickle each time the metal blade scraped the stone foundation and with chopped weeds raining from the sky at the apex of every slice, with itchy chaff sticking to arms and face, with every curse word I knew streaming from my chapped lips. In two years, I would be at Parris Island in July at Marine Corps boot camp where this exertion of adolescent angst would seem like a vacation. But I did not know that at the time. In thirty minutes, I reached the first corner, took a few deep breaths, turned east, and picked up my rhythm again.

Halfway down the east side my father's air conditioning compressor squirted out from the building. It stood on the ground, a square metal box of black rubber hoses and copper tubing partially obscured by a tall stand of mixed weeds. I swung away like a wild man staying as close to the unit as possible until I heard a snake-like hissing. A cloud of freon spurted upward, a gaseous geyser of catastrophic proportions that I knew my father would see as dollar signs escaping. And, he did. I won't go into much detail of the aftermath because it was only one of the many argumentative claims my father would be able to hold against me during my youth, and they all were basically the same. I was a careless, impulsive, reckless, teenager without something he called common sense. My restless, selfish behavior plagued him for years, but he was a good and generous man who forgave my erratic behavior on every occasion.

I'm not proud of my youthful indiscretions, or the discomfort those actions may have cost my family over the years. However, I suspect that most teenagers acted in a similar manner. It's been labeled many things by psychologists over centuries, but I can honestly relegate it to one very complicated process most of us live through called "growing up" full of too much testosterone. It's a condition that is hard to avoid.

What comes to me now after raising children of my own, after living a life full of all the joys and travails of being an enthusiastic, but often rash and thoughtless, human is an idea that we act without conscious bad intent sometimes based on unconscious desires, and it should cause us to question whether a bad result is an accident, or an unwillingness to examine our motives before we engage in questionable behavior. The idea that the swing of a sickle might be directed by an unconscious desire to fail spectacularly at this task did not cross my limited adolescent thinking ability. Certainly, it's more pleasant not to fully consider all aspects of actions before we act and easier to excuse some of our actions if we don't. But, is it better? I may never understand the answer to this question or know whether I was just a stupid boy or a mean-spirited boy. But considering these factors, even now, could make me a better human. That's a goal worth striving for.

The Myth of Fingerprints

Like many societies, we seem to be one that clamors for truth—in advertising, in news, in education, and in our relationships—but assume myth as an acceptable substitute because it's more comfortable and often provides answers for unanswerable questions. A myth, one agreed upon by a group of people or a society, is a product of an unproven perspective. A truth is factual regardless of perspective and is not swayed by unproven opinions. Take something as basic as fingerprints. The idea that fingerprints are unique to an individual is accepted as an absolute fact in most courts, but it has never been proven. On top of that, there are literally hundreds of different accepted standards for proving they match in courts all over the world. Those standards are administered from the perspectives of many human experts subject to all kinds of misinterpretations. Consequently, it is a proven fact that innocent people have been convicted of crimes based on faulty evidence and not necessarily truth.

Is it possible to separate truth from myth with any degree of consistency? Is one more important than the other in the development of a society or the nature of a culture? If so, which one and why? Certainly, one thing to consider is where it comes from. If a myth is generated by a trusted source, most of us are apt to believe it until faced with a personal reality we cannot deny, and sometimes that may be too late. For example, I never ate fish while drinking milk as a child and for much of my adulthood because my mother once told me that if I did, I would become dangerously ill as the combination of the two generated a severe form of poisoning called Toe Main. At some point in my reading history, I learned that spoiled fish created ptomaines and so did unpasteurized milk, but the combination of the two had nothing to do with either. Some foods are more likely than others to breed bacteria called ptomaine that can make you sick. These foods include: *Raw and undercooked foods from animals, including meat, chicken and other poultry, eggs, raw (unpasteurized) milk and products made from it, and seafood.* Then, I realized that somewhere in my mother's childhood someone ate fish and drank a glass of milk with it. One of them was spoiled and a myth was born that restricted my diet for decades, a minor discomfort.

However, on a grander scale, think of the myth generated by WWI and the Treaty of Versailles that ended it. This horrific slaughter was "the war to end all wars" and the peace that followed was intended to usher in an era of enlightenment and progress that would make the world a paradise forever after. At least that was the myth the Allied powers sold to the world. The reality proved to be quite different. The terms of the treaty crushed the people of Germany and left them desperate and starving to the extent that it generated Hitler's rise to power. Twenty years later, the world burned again.

Closer to home, the white people in America were spoon fed the idea of Manifest Destiny, a myth in the 19th century that allowed and encouraged them to believe that white, Eurocentric immigrants were destined to expand westward across the continent and fulfill a God-given right to own and prosper from the land. The belief was rooted in the mythology of the historical exceptionalism of the white race and a romantic nationalism it engendered. It was one of the earliest expressions of American imperialism by the United States, and while a great nation was built, it was built on the backs of slaves and the genocide of Native Americans with a bloody reality.

I'm not asking that you agree with everything I've written here, just consider it. The reason that myths have become so important in the 21st century, at least to me, is that we are governed by them because cable news generates and repeats them constantly now 24/7 for profit. We don't call them myths these days. The current phrase is "fake news" and while fake news is prevalent in every format like print news, advertising, education, and religion, it is most easily disseminated on

TV. What makes it so difficult to discern "fake news" may be tied to the reality that, like myths of old, it gives us the answers we need to alleviate personal anxiety while providing a comfortable narrative on which to base our preconceived opinions. Added to this is the reality that we have any number of choices from which to gather fake news whether our bias is liberal or conservative.

Here are some examples of how this works: All Muslims are terrorists, a myth as supported by false Focus News service – "Woman beheaded by Muslims in Oklahoma." We should stop people of color from immigrating to the U.S. comes from the myth as reported on Fox News called *replacement theory*, which says Democrats are allowing open borders so white people can be replaced by people of color who will vote for them. This one is tied to a reality that makes it believable to racists. In a few more decades whites will no longer be the majority race in this country due to demographic changes around the world, but it is not a ploy to secure more votes or to steal white jobs. I don't know any white person looking for migrant farm labor. Do you?

There is a movement in some states now to remove from education all history that is detrimental to the white race. This is currently being supported by the myth that slavery was beneficial for black people. Many liberals demand an end to the 2nd Amendment supported by a myth that gun ownership causes violent crime and argued against by conservatives who believe the myth that gun ownership is the only way a person can keep from being a victim. Both of these concepts are based on America's only unique mythology, that of the Wild West in the 19th century.

I could list many more ancient and well written mythologies. Consider the Greco-Roman gods like Zeus who use us for their own purposes. I haven't even considered the ten major world-wide religions. Most of them have Creation myths and apocalyptic flood myths. Many people of my generation died in Vietnam from the Domino Theory, prevalent nonsense provoked by intellectuals during the fifties and sixties based on the myth that all communism was a conspiracy created with the idea of world domination as its source. Mutually assured destruction, or MAD, initiated the building of thousands of missiles and nuclear warheads by the United States and Russia because of the myth that no one on either side would use nuclear bombs anymore if it meant the end of the world.

Whether a myth serves a positive purpose or a negative one depends on how it is used by people in power to manipulate the populations they govern. And, maybe more importantly, by how those populations receive that myth. If we accept it with blind credulity as fact because it makes us more comfortable, then a great danger arises that it will justify a destructive purpose for someone ultimately. If we research the history and purpose of the myth and discover the lessons and warnings it was developed symbolically to share, then there is a likelihood we may achieve something positive from its inclusion in our culture. This is on us. It is a responsibility we agreed to when we accepted self-governance by means of public education and the vote. The time has come for us to consider this while we can still claim to be free, especially before the next election.

Mardi Gras (circa 1971)

If you envision Mardi Gras as a time of surrealness with its parades, its King Cake, its orgasm of music and dance, its orgy of hedonistic pursuits, its blurring of the boundaries between reality and the world of shadows, then add the derangement of behavior by a thousandfold, and you may begin to glimpse its real intention—to remind us that human behavior never drifts too far from the current of insanity that flows through the mind of each and every human being. For some, we fight the fear of drowning in it. For others, the murky depths are a welcome respite from what society labels as normalcy. The Mardi Gras is the valve on a steam engine that lets humans blow off steam in an acceptable way for a week to avoid exploding unexpectedly at another time.

Although I spent a lot of time wandering the back alleys and shady bars of New Orleans in my youth, I attended only one Mardi Gras in my life, and it was enough. Bourbon street roiled with sweaty drunks packed so tightly that when one person tilted, thousands swayed as if connected to one large nervous system in the spine of a dancing leviathan. Every time I turned my head, the kaleidoscopic crowd changed form and colors.

"That guy might be God watching us sin," my friend Bill said, pointing at a mime with a flowing silver mane who struggled to escape an invisible box that seemed to be low on air. "Spoken like a true Irish Catholic." Considering Bill's point, I followed him down Bourbon Street, parting a curtain of jasmine, sewage, and stale beer with my drunken body. But it suddenly seemed too vivid for me, the smells, the embroidered western jackets, the sequins, the tie-dyed tee shirts and painted-on smiles. I began to wonder why I had come here. Then, as the alcohol from four Hurricanes dissipated in my blood stream, the question turned to existential dread, and my wonder took on a cosmic level. Why did anyone go anywhere at all?

In fear, I remembered something my alcoholic uncle once taught me. Once you start drinking, do not stop till you go to bed. Fortunately, both for my psyche and my budget, there was an oasis in the vestibule of a small apartment building. Two frat boys, entrepreneurs and business majors from Wichita State, had placed a board across cinder blocks and stocked their makeshift bar with bottles of cheap vodka, tequila, bourbon, and gin, which they sold in shots for fifty cents apiece. They owned one shot glass for community use, but AIDS was unknown in those days and the alcohol was close to kerosene in quality. No one complained about germs. After spending a buck and a half, I felt better.

Bill and I stumbled up one neon bright street and down another. What we found can be summed up in very few words—more of the same. Everywhere people laughed and drank. Like the first true native Americans, women sold their most prized possessions to rude white men for a few beads. The police kept their presence low key and friendly. Street hustlers tap danced and played harmonicas. I met a young black-haired beauty, and while Bill watched a Marilyn Monroe impersonator of dubious gender do a cabaret show, the girl took me for a taxi ride up Esplanade Avenue to St. Louis Cemetery next to Fairgrounds, the historically famous racetrack.

Ornate mausoleums guarded by sculptures of various angels and birds of prey seemed more like palaces than tombs. Unable to shake the strange electric current running at intervals through my stomach and up my spine, I felt as if I had entered a parallel reality, one where the invisible inhabitants were inviting me to stay. Pulling the girl close, I kissed her hard, more out of fear than lust. She responded, grinding her hips into mine. The cloying scents of vanilla and lilacs and honeysuckle made me dizzy.

"Not here," she whispered.

"I don't know your name."

"It isn't important in this place. All that matters is the mingling of our auras."

A sober, more experienced man might have exercised judgment rather than exorcised it. This was the point where I should have bolted for any exit, any source of light in the blackness swallowing us. She was speaking a paranormal language of the drug-dazed, crazy confused, and I was hearing a "please, fuck me" through the ears of the stupid.

"I have to call you something."

"Tonight, I shall be your muse. You shall enter a world that will inspire your dreams for years to come."

"How about Cindy? Cindy sounds good."

"You are on a journey with me and if you need me to be your Cindy, then your Cindy I shall be. Do you want one of these?"

Reaching into a small purse slung over her shoulder the girl, AKA Cindy, extracted a pearl pill container and held it toward me like the ciborium at a Catholic Mass, as if to offer communion to a repentant in dire need of salvation. From what, I had no idea, and I didn't take it. I didn't even look inside at the opened palm of her hand. But, considering the direction our conversation was traveling, it probably held mescaline or acid tabs.

"I'm good. No thanks." We entered a small stone crypt through an unlocked door. She sat, an offering, on the marble sarcophagus and leaned back. Extracting a candle from her purse, she lit the wick and holding it upside down let it drip hot wax on the surface until it pooled enough to hold the candle upright. Her flowered skirt billowed out over the sides of the tomb like an altar-cloth. In the flickering light, I noticed the pale, almost yellow glow of her cheeks, the aquiline angle of her nose and the thin pink lines of her lips stretched in more of a grimace than a smile. Sweat beaded across the high forehead and mascara dripped in rivulets from her black eyes. Pictures of a young Marie Laveau flooded my imagination. The turgid smell of freshly cut and dying lilies overwhelmed the hot, stale air. Hiking her skirt up, Cindy exposed what might be called a cornucopia of goodness to the cloying air and me. The visual nearness of my desired goal kept me focused enough to ignore the insanity.

"I never wear panties during Mardi Gras. I find them pretentious. Take me here at this point in the universe, I'm ready."

And she was, sort of. After much fumbling, scraping, knocking, unzipping, cursing, and tugging that substituted for foreplay while Cindy lay silent, I was able to mount a brief, uncomfortable offensive. Amid one of only a few strokes, she finally spoke.

"I hope he appreciates my efforts."

"He? He who?"

"My husband."

Anecdotes always circulated pool rooms and locker rooms of how some poor guy was humiliated to the point of flaccidity by a voracious woman. Now, I became aware that this instantaneous limpness mid-coitus could also be initiated by fear of a beating. I looked over my shoulder and out the opened door and saw only vague motionless shadows thrown by moonlight, marble, and cold stone gargoyles.

"What's wrong, darling boy," Cindy whispered.

"Where the fuck is he?"

"Who?"

"Your goddamn husband," I squealed. She chuckled slightly.

"We're on him. He died in a car crash three days ago. This is his final resting place. It has yet to be sealed."

I jumped up and stumbled a few steps backward. Unable to speak, I zipped my shriveled penis into my pants and began to rapidly walk away. I would have run, but my knees were too weak to carry the weight of my panic.

"Stop. We need your seed to consummate the ritual."

I heard her plea diminish with rapidly escalating distance. Who knows what ancient and dark ritual of ghoulish gothic witchcraft she practiced? Occultism was fast becoming another new drug for my Boomer generation. After all, Bill had just paid a mambo priestess to put a Voodoo curse on his unfaithful fiancé that very afternoon. Whether these attempts at communication with the spirit realm worked was another question. Although there were times in the jungles of Vietnam that some otherworldly luck seemed to keep me alive, I had no proof that it had been summoned for my specific protection. It appeared more like fog, drifting in and out of an event shrouding arbitrary people at capricious times.

Leaving Cindy sitting on the corpse of her husband in a kind of trance, I caught a taxi back to the Quarter. Evidently the look of terror on my face startled even the driver. He never said a word until I rode the few blocks. When the taxi stopped, he spoke. "Ride's on me boy. Pale as you is, I's ispect you better spend your money on whiskey."

Where What Is Lost Gets Found

"The simple joy he felt at being once more a part of such familiar things also contained an element of strangeness and unreality. With a sharp stab of wonder he reminded himself, as he had done a hundred times in the last few weeks, that he had really come home again —"

— Thomas Wolfe, from *You Can Never Go Home Again*

When I was asked to contribute an essay in this edition of the Indiana Historical Society's *Traces* magazine regarding how I came back and what I found had changed after my tour of duty in Vietnam, what had changed could be described in one word, *innocence*, and I mean my own. I had disappeared, which sounds simple and not very profound. Every teenager loses their innocence, usually by small increments and specific circumstances over a long period of time that stretches from entering puberty through getting a job, getting married, having children, buying a home, and basically learning to deal with adult issues. Children become men and women, and the changes are acceptable because they are buffered by the passage of years.

However, in a war that passage from childhood to adulthood comes in days, hours, minutes and for some it happens in an instant. Consequently, what you come home to is a world that is the same, but different, than the one you left. It isn't because your hometown geography changed radically, or the people you had known all your young life developed new attitudes regarding country, flag, patriotism, God, or family. Things remain pretty much the same for the most part in the few years you are absent. The change occurs quite simply in your mind because you aren't the person who left. Thoughts before you left of a future career, marriage, and a stable life that you may have had in high school got replaced by one overriding concern twenty-four hours a day for seven days a week—survival. Upon your return that survival morphs into a series of confusing questions. How am I still alive? Why am I still alive when men closer to me than brothers died at my side? What will I do with all this existence I've been granted but don't deserve? Who am I?

Consider the small Southern Indiana town called Princeton that was my home for arguably the most important first eighteen years of my life. This was the place, and these were the people, beyond my parents and teachers, that formed a masculine code and a rural American value system for me, a town that had come to represent my understanding of the entire world. That's an important point. Princeton, Indiana, and the life therein, was pretty much my entire context for reality before I enlisted in the Marine Corps. Because of that context, *I would have been embarrassed not to enlist.* Yes, it's probably a lot more complex psychologically for those of you inclined to analyze decisions and actions, but that is the bottom line. I was an impulsive teenager.

Many small towns rose from the rich farm soil of the Ohio Valley from a basic idea—symmetry. Symmetry of one kind or another was a human concept that permeated every aspect of the environment molded by human hands in our county as if evenness and balance were always the same thing. My town had been crowned as the county seat, a royal privilege that required every part of it to set a symmetric example. The town grew in squares from a single square. Out of an airplane window you could look down and see a series of perfect blocks expanding from the center on all sides. One square divided into another like cells of a living organism until the people stopped building and an even perimeter formed the city limits on all sides.

Two main roads ran in and out of town east and west, and two ran north and south. The points where they intersected formed a center and traffic lights hung on each of the four corners. The county courthouse, an imposing four-story edifice of red brick and concrete, rose majestically, topped by a spire that housed a bell tower and four giant clock faces, one in each direction. The bell hanging in the tower struck a piercing metallic toll exactly at hourly intervals, one for every hour, to signify the passage of time, a necessary ritual due to one hour being very much like the past hour and very much like the next. It was a minor annoyance unless you lived close to the town square at midnight and were awakened rudely from a drunken slumber.

Inside this austere building all the county political and administrative functions were carried out with due diligence by judges, clerks, lawyers, two janitors, and military recruitment officers from each of our national branches of service. Opposite and across the street of each directional face of the courthouse, local businesses that would one day be ruined by a Walmart and drive-thru fast-food companies on the west side of town, enjoyed prosperity—two jewelry and clothing stores, two Five & Dime shops, Demoss Rexall Drugs, a shoe store, and a J.C. Penney's. The dystopian urban sprawl that began to destroy them was at least a decade away in 1963. My favorite establishment and the favorite of all boys suffering the pangs of pubescent angst was The Palace Pool Room that rested next to the Gibson County Bank building.

The Palace was a combination diner, sports den, gambling room, billiards parlor, and news hub for the male population of the county. Women never entered this sweaty domain that stank of cigar smoke and pool chalk during the 1950's and most of the 1960's, and we were therefore not subjected to the social awkwardness of our own self-conscious paranoia in their presence. It was the perfect place to grow from an immature boy to an immature man and exactly where I found myself at noon on Friday, November 22nd of that year.

Even though it was a school day, my being here was not unusual. The high school was only three blocks west of the town square, and I often walked there during my lunch break. One dollar would buy a coney island at the Palace—a hotdog topped with chili sauce, onions, and ground beef— and an order of fries and a coke. Most days I spent my lunch money among the denizens that provided me with early examples of manhood and the behavior that would be expected from me as I grew older.

Actually, my loss of innocence began with bird crap. The county courthouse clock tower and the eaves of its roof provided perfect space and shelter for nesting, and my town was one of those rural farm towns that was blessed with fodder for every species of bird from starlings to chicken hawks, but particularly pigeons. Pigeons attacked the clock tower frequently, building an elaborate series of feathered hostels. Hundreds roosted in cracks and crevices along the gutters. Pigeon droppings painted the town square with white and black dots. The flying grey rats dive-bombed lawyers, the old circuit judge, the county clerk, and the beehive hairdos of her all-female staff. Even the credit criminals could not dodge the reign of terror as they snuck into a court. These winged demons held no regard for status or beauty. They eliminated their loads on Cadillac's and Chevy's alike. They defaced park benches and Civil War statues.

Enough was enough. The mayor phoned our county game warden who arrived on this day with a half dozen shotguns loaded with bird shot and a coffee thermos. We, the miscreants of misogyny, crowded against the plate glass window to watch. The pigeons were no match for our uniformed gladiator, although it did seem that his "Smokey-the-Bear" hat got splattered once or twice. For thirty minutes the sky filled with smoke and cordite. It rained feathers and blood. The air stank of bird entrails as shotgun blasts rattled shop windows and merchants ran outside their businesses carping like scalded dogs. Pigeon parts were carted off the sidewalks by a gang of feral cats. We onlookers became filled with bloodlust, breaking our silence and cheering as the body count rose.

I was ambivalent as regards hunting, a rite of passage for every red-blooded male in Gibson County, but felt uncomfortable with all the bird murder. However, I did not want to be embarrassed. So, as the cacophony of cheers filled the airy room, I joined the choir and soon became as jaded to violence as the rest. With all the noise, no one heard Walter Cronkite on the black and white TV above the lunch counter as he described the noon motorcade of our popular President JFK and his wife, the beautiful Jackie. The line of cars snaked slowly around the square in Dealey Plaza as the couple in the open convertible waved to the Dallas, Texas, crowd and smiled.

My innocence took its first jolt that day. From that point onward through this avian slaughter, the murder of a president, race riots in Watts, the Boston Strangler, the escalation of violence in Vietnam, the brutal murder of three Civil Rights workers in Mississippi, and the commitment of thousands of troops to an ever-expanding war effort in Southeast Asia, the world seemed to implode in the next four years.

The daily conversation in the Palace Pool Room ping-ponged between these events and others, but the gist of the discussions rested on the fact that every teen-aged male in our town needed to do his part in controlling these atrocities by fighting the world-wide takeover being attempted by "Commies." Vietnam appeared to be the only place we could stop them. Therefore, by 1967 it had become my duty to enlist. *I was embarrassed not to.*

After travelling ten thousand miles and warring against these "Commies," I returned home in 1969 wounded, full of shrapnel, scarred inside and out with the life-altering questions mentioned earlier burning a hole in me large enough for my soul to leak out. How am I still alive? Why am I still alive when men closer to me than brothers died at my side? What will I do with all this existence I've been granted, but don't deserve? Who am I?

I can't honestly say the town changed physically much while I was gone. The weather remained much the same, the highest daily average was 98 degrees in August and the lowest was 18 degrees in February.

However, there were a few. My high school had been rechristened Princeton Community High due to its consolidation with smaller county schools. Princeton native Dave Thomas, a frequent visitor of Greek's Candy Shop, had moved away and opened his first Wendy's in Columbus, Ohio. The high school band with Steve King as drum major finished 25th in state competition, and the Gibson County Fair, a staple in Princeton since 1851, featured an expanded entertainment lineup; Roy Acuff, The Ink Spots, King Kovaz Auto Thrill Show, various high school bands, the Fair Queen Contest, Carnaby Street USA dance pavilion (dances every night Monday thru Saturday), Harness Racing, Tractor Pulling Contest, 4-H and open Class Displays, and Wacky Jackie the Clown. Oak and Maple trees bloomed along the narrow streets that led to the fairgrounds. The churches filled with families on Sunday mornings and life continued at its leisurely pace much as it had before I left to fight a war in 1967.

With that said, there was an undercurrent of transformation in the American Dream beginning in Princeton, a small but noticeable tension to someone whose perception had been altered so radically as mine. Some WWII veterans, like my father, had begun to question the necessity and validity of purpose regarding our involvement in Vietnam, especially since boys from well-known families had died there. My personal friends from high school, Bob Staley and Billy Lynn were killed between 1968-69. High school boys began to voice strong concern at the possibility of being drafted into the military, and many parents encouraged them to enter college or seek other deferments after reality that the draft could be a death sentence hit so close to home. And, I noticed the prevalence of marijuana over Falls City Beer at some parties at camps along the White and Wabash rivers. The Summer of Love, which was born in 1967 in San Francisco, finally arrived with long hair and bellbottomed jeans for teenagers in Princeton around 1969 to the consternation of many parents.

None of these changes was catastrophic for the foundation of conservative, Christian values that shrouded rural Southern Indiana in a cocoon of patriotism, but it did create in me confusion and an uncertainty about my own definition of normalcy, or at least what I thought I had to get back to after so many months of life in a violently abnormal situation. Oh, I tried. Like thousands of other veterans who returned to an unfamiliar familiarity in hundreds of other small towns. Some of them it back, and I attempted to insert myself into that environment for a while. Failing miserably at a middleclass lifestyle, I kept struggling. I joined a local church, played in a local slo-pitch softball league, tried to learn bridge, and rekindled some old friendships with people who had no idea how to even converse with me about my recent past experiences. It didn't work well, and a few months after my return, I left again.

What I'm describing was not a unique experience. Many people across America, old and young alike, were shifting from almost religious acceptance of the sacrosanct proverb uttered by a hero of the War of 1812, Stephen Decatur—"My country, right or wrong, my country"—to a question raised by my father's friend that I overheard in a heated argument during a poker game at the Elks Club. "What the hell are we doing over there anyway?"

This subtle shift in attitude among a few former staunch believers was perhaps for me the greatest change in my hometown, and one that I could not reconcile in my own mind by remaining in a place where I found no answer. I spent the next decade as a wanderer, travelling across the country working hard labor and listening to the same argument in many other cities, large and small, till the excesses of the 1960's and 1970's reached its apex, and I found the answers to all my questions were inside me. That's when I really came home.

Character

I am a Fogey, Fuddy-duddy, Geezer, Dinosaur, Fossil, or literally, an old man. I entered high school in 1962. It was the end of one era and the beginning of another. To quote Charles Dickens, "It was the best of times, it was the worst of times." To paraphrase Hunter Thompson, things were starting to get fucked up. The idea that education should be politically correct, and nurturing was still unheard of. Corporal discipline meant to instill character in seemingly irredeemable teenage boys was encouraged as a necessary evil to check the surge of testosterone flooding our bodies.

For example, walking the hall one day I saw Mr. Sparks, the math teacher who was a decent fellow and what some might call an egghead, a rather quiet and erudite man. Out of character, he flailed his arms back and forth and up and down to punctuate an animated discussion with a burly senior class boy named Joe. Joe dwarfed Mr. Sparks who was tiny and light, like a ragged scarecrow picked at by crows and losing straw at weird points on his body. Think Dorthy's travelling companion in Oz. On the other hand, Joe stood almost six feet tall with thick lips, light reddish hair, a ruddy complexion and weighed close to two hundred pounds. He was thickly muscled, smiled mischievously, and his eyes held a constant Irish twinkle. Think giant mutant leprechaun.

For an eighteen-year-old, the senior held a reputation like an ancient mythical warrior. It was said Joe got drunk one Saturday night at Lamey's Grove—a popular dance hall for the rowdy under-legal-age drinking crowd—and when the security guards attempted to remove him, he whipped five of them like stray dogs. It was said he whipped two state troopers who stopped his car on the highway while in handcuffs and after drinking a keg of beer. It was said he feared no man or beast and had once bent a lug wrench with his hands when angry. This was the danger facing timid Mr. Sparks on the staircase when the bell rang, and we all rushed to change classrooms.

I wondered why the math teacher made an issue of Joe running up the stairs even if walking was all the principal allowed. The teacher stood on the landing between floors. He reached out and grabbed Joe's left shirt sleeve as Joe, ignoring him, turned to leave. All in one motion, Joe whirled, shot out both hands against Mr. Sparks' chest, lifting him off his feet and sending him backwards down a flight of steps. Luckily, the fellow bounced on his ass and off several students, buffering the violent descent.

Enter Clayton Weist, our high school principal. Mr. Weist—yes, I still call him Mister out of respect, even though he died many years ago. He witnessed the incident from across the hallway. In three long strides, he had hapless Joe by the shirt collar. Hauling him across the hardwood, he hurled Joe into his office and slammed the door. The frosted glass in the top half rattled and trembled but did not break. From that moment forward, the whole incident was on audio. I saw nothing, but the sounds coming from behind that door were self-explanatory. The thumping, clanging, bumping and banging, maybe even a whimper or two, had stopped all commotion in the hallway. We were supposed to be changing classrooms but stared at the closed door, mesmerized as if standing on a streetcorner observing a car wreck.

You see, Mr. Weist got his straight bearing and authoritative tone as a colonel in the army, becoming an educator only after retirement. Not only was he used to demanding obedience from guys much tougher than Joe, Mr. Weist was capable of earning the respect of guys much tougher than Joe. When I told my father about the incident, he just laughed and said, "You really have to be some kind of stupid to try Weisty's patience. I remember when he was a student himself before he joined the army. He worked the oil fields in southern Illinois to earn money during the summer. Weisty wasn't afraid of much, but he had a rabid fear of snakes. One of the older guys on the rig found a harmless blacksnake and threw it on him as a joke. He shook that snake off, took a deep breath, and smacked that guy across the head with an iron pipe. No words were spoken and no one played any more pranks on him that summer."

I have no proof that any of the stories about Joe or our principal were true, but I do know what I saw. Joe left Mr. Weist visibly shaken. He always had a pale complexion like many redheads, but leaving that office, his face looked as if it had been dipped in bleach. Not only that, I heard that Mr. Sparks received a sincere apology.

Most stories, especially true ones, have a moral or a point to make. Mine is obvious, I think. We live in an era when all the hard years and hard work a person goes through to become a teacher earns no respect. Teachers get paid very little compared to the long hours they put in at school and at home doing their jobs. Their opinions don't mean anything, even in their fields of expertise, to "helicopter" parents who hover at school board meetings and complain that their children are being made uncomfortable by learning FACTS that don't coincide with personal opinions. A teacher has no options for disciplining a smart-ass teenager who disrupts class constantly without risking job termination or an assault charge.

I'm not making a case here for a return to corporal punishment. If Mr. Weist was to manhandle Joe these days, he'd be jailed for assault even if Joe deserved it. Also, it's too easy for humans to abuse power instead of directing it toward a constructive end. I'm saying that learning anything requires that a student is made uncomfortable sometimes. I'm wishing parents would help instill manners and consideration and the value of critical thinking at home instead of entitlement and privilege in their offspring. I know it's difficult to raise children, especially during adolescence. I raised some myself.

Something more difficult happens if we don't instill the value of being taught where we are at as a society and how we got here and communicate respect for the people tasked with teaching these things, exactly what most professional educators are trained to do. This applies especially in the field of humanities (i.e. history, literature, culture, art, philosophy, sociology, debate, etc.) because this is the education—the learning of how to live together—that makes a society possible. If you think I'm wrong, read the newspaper headlines. How are we doing these days since parents begin fighting facts being taught? In some southern states, slavery cannot be spoken of in school. It must be called "The Atlantic Trade Triangle." What really caused Custer's last stand? What American foreign policy screw up led to the war in Vietnam? What noticeable scientific advancements came from ethnic minorities? How has corporate interest influenced our economic development for workers? Why did the Founding Fathers express distrust of religion in government? Who deserves the right to vote and why? Has the Constitution always been correct (ex. Blacks were once considered only 3/5's human by law)? Should we ban great works of literature because a phrase from the past in them may "trigger" our precious babies? Every one of these questions, among many other delicate ones, is important to all our citizens in understanding ways to make life better for all of us. That has always been a major goal of public education.

That type of teaching and learning can't be done without some level of discipline and some respect for the people who have chosen to sacrifice their time and energy doing it because it requires challenging pre-conceived notions and myths that we have often taken for truth. Parents can't abdicate this responsibility at home, require it from professionals, and then complain when they do it. When we do, we instill the idea in our children that their own opinions and bias and prejudicial attitudes, which they learn from us, will always outweigh facts. It will also make life harder for them when they enter a world where no one else cares what they think, but only what they have learned.

Balance

In 1969, I tried to come home after fighting a brutal war against a tiny nation of people because my government decided the idea of communism was a bad idea for everybody in the entire world. My body traveled back to Indiana, back to corn fields and county fairs, baseball and freckled farm girls tied to the wrists of future farmers, bouncy like helium balloons. I took a job at my father's auto dealership selling cars. He had visions of me taking over the business one day. I attended church on Sundays with family. People patted me on the back, called me hero, patriot. The president of the little league asked me to coach a team. The guy remembered that I had played well for my high school team and thought that a war hero would be a great example for twelve-year old's what with all the anti-war parents starting to show up at the games where once there were only patriots and maybe America would need more soldiers when these kids were old enough.

It was fun for a while. The ball field spread out directly across the street from St. Joe's where I attended mass every Sunday. I enjoyed my little ballplayers, and the team won more games than it lost during the season. I was reminded of a better time in my own life, a time that seemed far away now but was in fact less than two years ago. Some of the parents seemed over-anxious and too competitive, but happy as long as the team kept winning. My body felt almost well till the end of summer when the boys played for the league championship on the last weekend. That's when I began to think maybe my mind wasn't. Maybe my mind hadn't come back from the war, and I didn't know why not.

But this was fourteen years before anyone acknowledged the existence of Post Traumatic Stress Disorder for Vietnam veterans. After all, we only had to be in a combat area for a year if we could survive. That tour of duty was nothing compared to the three and a half years my father spent in the European Theatre with the 82nd Airborne in WWII. No one bothered to calculate the actual time spent in combat *conditions* for that conventional war was sixty-five days a year compared to two hundred and eighty days a year for the war we were fighting. It certainly never crossed my mind at the time, or if it did all it felt like was the vague gnawing sensation of failure in my stomach.

The dog days of August cast a shimmer of heat and humidity over the diamond. It was our most important game, according to a few of the parents. I felt no urgency one way or the other. I simply enjoyed being distracted from his own thoughts for an afternoon. The first three innings came and went without much action. Timmy Milson, my best pitcher, seemed to have the opposite team's batters mesmerized with his fastball. Timmy had grown faster than most of the other boys and was almost as tall as me. He threw hard, but his control was often erratic. That had two benefits. Many hitters swung and missed a bad pitch but remained timid and afraid of the good ones. Consequently, the opposing team's batting lineup stayed off balance. If not for rules to protect a young pitcher's arm, I would have pitched the Milson kid every game.

With the score tied at 1-1 and two men out, Timmy threw a fastball that got away from him. It tailed high and hard into a slender kid even though the kid had backed away from the plate and stood on the edge of the batter's box. A loud thump echoed across the field as the ball hit the side of the batter's plastic helmet. An audible collective gasp as if a balloon was leaking air rose from the bleachers on both sides of the field. The batter went down. He didn't jerk backward or stumble forward, he simply collapsed like something turned his bones into jelly.

I ran onto the field. The umpire ripped off his mask and stepped toward the injured boy bundled across home plate. Concerned parents moved toward the high fence behind home plate. Chaos built in the stands, but the other young players stood quietly, shifting from foot to foot or staring into the palms of their ball gloves. Timmy smirked and I wanted to smack him for it.

Then, the glare of the sun on the blanched, dusty diamond, the shouts of panic from the batter's parents, and the sight of a medical tech entering the area made a nervous tic is my left eye come back. A wave of sadness swallowed me, dark and omnipresent, without context. After that day. I drank more whiskey and stayed out late at night. Coming in hungover and late for work several times in the next couple of weeks forced my father to threaten me with firing. What kind of a person gets fired by their own father? Parents complained about me cursing in front of the boys at the league banquet. Something I didn't even realize I'd done. My family home became a place where days were spent remembering things no one wants to remember.

Sitting in my mother's kitchen, drinking more cheap whiskey and grasping for some boundary, after reaching for some liturgy to chant or Eucharist other than bourbon to swallow, finding no way at twenty-one years of age to understand the sacrifice of war or even bring sanity inside the empty sound of a spring rain, I realized that something was wrong inside me, but not what, as if one of the many gears that drove the machine somewhere inside my head had chipped a gear. The whirring hum of contentment became a whine and a clang. My thoughts lost any sort of focus and no matter how much I drank, sleep became impossible. If only I could have left them all, the dead ones, in their graves below their stone monuments scarred with carved letters and the tears of their children, unborn and unnamed. After convincing my mother, sister, and brother I was alright, I admitted to myself I was not. The admission terrified me. My sanity seemed to be slipping away in nights of sleeplessness.

Explaining my need for new experiences to my father was impossible. He had come home from a war, married, worked steady and hard, and raised a family. Packing my Marine Corps duffel bag with the few civilian clothes I owned, a chipped Currier and Ives shaving mug, and a dog-eared copy of *Trout Fishing in America*, taking what little money I had managed to not waste, I ran, or rather drove, in a used Dodge pick-up truck, drifting south down Highway 41 toward the Mississippi Delta. My mother cried a little and wrung her arthritic hands as I backed the truck down the driveway, but she seemed to accept the fact that the son who left for the Middle East was not the one who returned, but not that I needed to work my way from the edge of life toward the center. After driving for ten hours straight jacked up on No-Doz and nicotine, I arrived at the longest bridge over a body of water in the whole United States.

The sign read Lake Pontchartrain, but it was a lie. Pontchartrain was a causeway not a lake and sixty percent sea water. But the people of New Orleans wanted it to be a lake and refused to call it anything else. After a time, the whole world came to see this body of water the same way. Any place that had enough voodoo magic in words spoken by its residents to change tangible nature had to be a place where I could correct my past.

Vieux Carre, bon temps, Café du Monde...I loved pronouncing the words incorrectly with a Midwestern twang, especially when I got drunk. They sounded so much more exotic than *French Quarter*. From my first night in New Orleans onward, I managed to maintain a euphoria brought on by cheap drinks and flashing neon lights. Anything seemed possible in this place of no rules, so long as it related to one of the five senses. I ate heroes and po-boys, crawfish and raw oysters, red beans & rice, and gumbo. I drank hurricanes without restraint, grabbed ass in the strip joints on Bourbon Street without regard to gender, saw children tap-dancing in the street, pissed on alley walls, teased the mimes in Jackson Square, and heard music twenty-four hours a day whether it was being played or not. It was a smokey, deep, honest music called the blues. I felt its raw, repetitive power. Time hung suspended, trapped between beignets for breakfast and cocktails for dinner. In the raucous laughter of all night revelers, in a place where the illusion of a party was constant even if unreal, I found sanctuary. I was Quasimodo hidden high in the tower of Notre Dame, dancing among the pealing bells.

It lasted four days. On the morning of the fifth day, I woke up in a place called Poppy's Diner. Exhausted, hungover, and hungry at 3:00 a.m., I lifted a groggy head from the table and searched my pockets for a few dollars to buy food. No one seemed to notice my presence, or care. A thin cook steamed burgers beneath a dented hubcap on a smoking grill. The sweet scent of sage and cayenne quickened my pulse. Hunger of one kind or another always made that happen.

Glancing around the room, my bleary gaze settled on the Marilyn Monroe impersonator sitting by the window. He was a beautiful boy I had noticed before performing at a Bourbon Street sex club—hair the color of corn silk and thick, pouty, crimson lips. The boy had a perfect chocolate mole on a satin cheek and wore the exact replica of Marilyn's white sleeveless dress from *Some Like it Hot*.

When the boy smiled, I smiled back, feeling something between curiosity and sadness. A thickly muscled, black-haired fellow wearing a white shirt with a black bow tie and instantly recognizable as the Cajun bartender from the Napoleon House entered the place and walked directly to the Wurlitzer juke box. Dropping in a quarter, he played a Clifton Chenier Fais Do Do and turned to the Boy Marilyn.

"Bon soir chere. Voulez-vous danser?"

The cook lifted the hubcap and flipped the burger underneath it. The dazed boy rose, hesitated and, as a drop of sweat dripped from the cook's brow, swooned into the outstretched arms. The bartender waltzed the boy around the floor, gliding between tables politely. In my wonderment at the surreal scene playing out in front of me, I became part of it. The dancers tilted, spun, and sputtered like a slowing top that wobbles but refuses to collapse. I clapped my hands and stomped my foot to the Fais Do-Do rhythm. The soft breeze roused by their twirling gently lifted the hem of the white dress, exposing a beautiful pair of shaved legs. I tried to stay in time but began to feel dizzy. Was it from the dance, or my hunger? The slide of worn leather over sawdust generated a damp panic. When the song ended and the couple kissed, I swore the hint of salt mingled with the taste of warm flesh on my own lips.

I ate two cheeseburgers and drank coffee till well past sunrise. The Cajun and his movie star had long since departed, as did most of the other pre-dawn customers, replaced now by a different crowd of working stiffs. They came for scrambled eggs and Louisiana hot sauce, maybe chicory coffee and fried beignets, before punching a time clock in some boutique or voodoo shop or adult bookstore, anywhere tourists would congregate and relinquish their money with a little coaxing. Remembering I was almost out of cash myself, I needed gainful employment somewhere, and I wanted a job anywhere because I needed to stay lost. The problem was I had no skills, only the conditioning and discipline to run ten miles without getting winded and the ability to field strip an M-16 in less than a minute. My hand trembled from the long night of gin when I reached into my pocket and extracted several quarters. The coins clattered against the coffee saucer as I tossed them on the table for a tip and, returning a nod from the cook, walked out the front door.

Outside in the bright Delta sun, I collided with the world. Parting a curtain of smells woven from jasmine incense, sewage, stale beer, and bacon, I stopped on the corner of St. Ann and Jackson Square to buy a Times Picayune from a vendor. It was getting all too vivid, this funk of life and bad love and hedonism. There had to be more to New Orleans than tourist traps. There had to be work. Nauseous, I sat on a bench and opened the paper to the classifieds.

Above the crinkling pages, hucksters hawked their wares in the square. According to them, no one should be without a caricature drawing, balloon, doll, straw hat, photograph, or original painting of the Quarter, some souvenir to remind people when they had last been free of responsibility, free to enjoy their senses and, most importantly, free to spend their money. Glancing over the top of the want ads, I noticed a mime running through his routine for some children and their parents. The mime pretended to be locked in a box, imprisoned in a world he couldn't feel or see. The more I watched the animated gestures and the expression of panic on the mime's white-painted face, the more the terror seemed contagious. My nausea grew to epic proportions and the bile rose in my throat. It was a hangover from four days of gin and spicy food, the shedding of a former self, and the spinning, whirling rush of living that would drive me in multi-directional chaos for many years and to many places, through a half-dozen failed relationships and more failed careers.

It took me three more decades and five years of therapy courtesy of the Veterans Administration to understand what the driving force in my life had been for all those chaotic years. It was the power of guilt. The facts of surviving intense trauma as others around me didn't, the knowledge that I was capable of instant, horrible violence, and the realization that corruption of morality could occur even with good intentions threw my entire being off balance. I had to relearn and correct my assumptions of what it meant to be a human being. This sounds simple when I say it, but the doing of that, the struggle to find balance and the discipline to maintain may be the most difficult requirement in our lives. More importantly in our lives together.

Worthy

Chester, New York, spills off the Palisades Parkway about seventy miles northwest of New York City. It rests, like Rip Van Winkle, in the foothills of the Catskill Mountain Range. When I first moved there after returning from the Vietnam War, the town and surrounding countryside was in the process of explosive change.

Generations of Dutch and German immigrants had built huge dairy farms broken up only by acres of pine forests, stone fences, and lazy streams. White barns stood beside white homes at the end of shaded lanes. The whole area had been a pastoral postcard for over two hundred years.

Then, a generation of farmers went off to Europe and fought the Nazis. Those who lived to return home made the mistake of having children. The post-war baby boomer generation cultivated no patience for milking cows. Upon inheriting the land, they parsed it off to developers. Former farms and wild forests evolved into a sort of prefab suburbia.

Hundreds of New York City cops, firemen, sanitation workers, and low-level bureaucrats began to move their families into these aluminum-sided shells hoping to escape the hard drugs, random violence, frenetic pace, and high price of urban living. For many of them, grass was an acrid weed rolled in cigarette paper and smoked. They had no idea what country living entailed, only that it was cheaper and less dangerous than city living for their families.

Expectations, aggravated by the loss of identity for both groups of people, the ones who grew up in Chester and the ones who moved there, created an atmosphere of chaos and culture shock.

A mile outside Chester and fenced off from the confusion a formidable cluster of concrete and steel buildings rose from the black earth. It was born as a women's prison early in the twentieth century and with the idea that an institution of rehabilitation should be self-sufficient. In order to give the debauched and degraded female felons opportunities for learning job skills, the prison operated a vegetable farm, a canning factory for preparing the produce, and a train station to ship it off to commercial markets. However, like puberty, the depression created an obnoxious adolescent from its infant enterprise, a product consumers neither wanted nor could afford. The business of exploiting captive labor soon went belly up and the prisoners were moved to prisons with less overhead in other parts of the state.

After years of abandonment, the Department of Social Services in New York City came up with a solid plan to recoup the city's investment. Interestingly, the idea coincided with the onset of social security payments to the elderly and the disabled. They sent out the municipal medical vans. Paramedics scooped up the ill and wretched and homeless alcoholics who lay around the alleyways in the Bowery, depositing them in the detox center on 3rd Street.

Here, the men who were consumed and ravaged by their addiction went through delirium tremors and a number of other problems, any of which could be classified as a major health crisis, until they were steady enough to sign a form. The form allowed the city to apply for social security benefits on their behalf and collect the money for as long as the men were interned somewhere and attempts were made at rehabilitation. Enter the former women's prison at Chester, New York, now remade into the benevolent Camp LaGuardia.

Dried out dregs of humanity got bussed constantly from the city to the country. Some men stayed a few weeks, some a few months, and some remained there until they died making pottery, walking the spacious grounds, drinking the bad coffee, and eating three square meals a day. The camp was always full and always in need of "aides" to watch over its inhabitants.

Having majored in sociology during the short time spent in college before enlisting in the Marine Corps and almost completing the degree after I got out, I knew a little something about this kind of "service to society" work, and I needed a job desperately for two reasons. The last of my savings was disappearing, and I felt the need to atone in some way for participating so enthusiastically in the Vietnam debacle. At the ripe old age of twenty-four, *everything* is not enough. The nightmares, the chaos, and the burgeoning symptoms of Post Traumatic Stress Disorder didn't count as repentance.

Not having finished that degree work in sociology meant The New York Department of Social Services could hire me at a salary barely above minimum wage. I became the perfect candidate for the opening labeled "recreational therapist" listed in the Chester local newspaper. So, I drove to Camp LaGuardia hoping for employment.

Slightly apart from the cluster of rectangular buildings, a squat, square, gray one labeled "Administration" stood before me in the midst of Camp LaGuardia. Everything about it seemed hard and slightly intimidating, like the warden's office it had been. As I stepped from the car, an elderly man flailed his hands at a huge tree, ranting in what seemed to be gibberish, but was, I learned later, Polish. In fact, the grizzled orator in a stocking cap and navy pea coat believed himself to be the ambassador from Poland. He reported to the tree every morning after breakfast, believing it to be the general assembly of the United Nations.

Inside the building behind a glass wall, a receptionist named Rosemarie frowned at me and pointed to the visitors' register. After signing my name, she ushered me into the camp director's office to be interviewed. For some reason, which seemed odd to me, no one else waited to lay claim on this job. Was I the only person in Chester who saw the altruistic and economic potential inherent here? Was I the only unemployed veteran in New York?

A large gray man sat behind a metal desk. He pointed and waved me indifferently into a wooden chair. The air in the office was a pale blue tint, almost the color of fresh milk after the yellow cream has been skimmed off. Clouds of cigarette smoke floated upward, sucked toward and then twirled around a squeaky ceiling fan. The smells of ashes, English Leather, sweat, and newspaper ink swirled around in the slight breeze created by the fan. The director lit a Camel, adding to the cloud cover. The nameplate on the desk read *Roger Peckinpaugh.*

"Mr. Peckinpaugh?"

The balding black man with light, amber colored skin looked beyond me as Rosmarie backed out and shut the door.

"Call me Director. Why are you here?"

"I'm here for a job interview, Director."

"What's your name?"

"McGarrah. Jim McGarrah."

"Well, McGarrah, what makes you think you're qualified for this job? We take our work seriously here."

The director frowned and I didn't know quite how to respond. In reality, I knew nothing about the treatment of alcoholism or psychotherapy, even less about administration of a social program. Peckinpaugh released the frown into a broad grin.

"Just kidding," he said. "If you can sit in one spot, watch a bunch of Bowery bums make pottery, listen to their sad stories, which are all basically the same, of life gone bad and not lose your own mind, you'll be perfect for the job."

Over the next several months Roger Peckinpaugh became my first major example of how mediocre bureaucrats put the Peter Principle into solid action.

He lit another cigarette and shooed me from the room as dispassionately as he had waved me in. Rosemarie stood with her elbows propped on a long marble counter, staring out the window into a vast open area filled with broken men who milled around aimlessly like cattle in a stockyard.

"I got hired. I'll be here to sign in at seven-thirty in the morning."

"Big surprise. We'll see how long you last."

Hair on the back of my neck rose slightly, and blood rushed to my head. My hands tingled. I had joined the great American workforce, my first attempt at a normal life since the war. I came to work the next morning and, after a brief orientation session, was assigned to supervise the men who spent their waking hours in the train station. Peckinpaugh gave me the title of "Recreational Therapist" and ignored me from that first day forward.

The old train station where women used to load canned vegetables on boxcars before returning to their cells had been converted into a recreational facility by the addition of a couple of kilns for baking ceramic ashtrays and strange glazed birds, a newspaper press for publishing a camp newspaper, and a few woodworking benches complete with primitive tools.

Initially, I took my job seriously and did my best to rehabilitate my charges. I had always been a little like a Quarter horse, exploding from the starting gate at a dead run and gasping for air a quarter mile up the track. This personality characteristic traveled with me wherever I went, and each job I took got my total devotion and energy for at least several weeks. Consequently, I began seeing the men at Camp LaGuardia not as they were, but as how I imagined them to have been, or worse, how I imagined they might be with my help. They told me stories of their downfalls, and I envisioned returning them to their glory, staying with them past quitting time and laboring late into the night to devise new recreational therapies.

The Ivy League professor who had become a Bowery bum brought my explosive start to a winded halt at Camp LaGuardia in record time. I begged him to tell me the reason he fell from such a lofty perch. Day after day, I looked into his dead eyes, the color of impenetrable turquoise. Day after day, he pushed his black-rimmed glasses, taped at the bridge, high up on his crooked nose and simply replied, "It was a matter of decorum for the provost."

A pudgy man, the professor spent most of his time at a corner table rolling cigarettes from Bugler tobacco and Tops rolling papers. He preferred Tops papers to the cheaper ones that came in the Bugler package. Those were his one extravagance. He would have preferred to continue smoking Nat Sherman Luxury Cigarettes, but the city of New York took his disability check directly from Social Security for room and board every month and credited him with five dollars at the canteen run by the camp to purchase toothpaste, shaving cream, soap, and any other so-called necessities that he could afford. The outrageous price of one dollar and fifty cents a pack for fancy smokes was beyond his reach economically, especially at a two-pack a day habit. So, he sat with his constant companion, a near famous hairdresser of near famous people from Greenwich Village. Ostensibly, they worked on the camp newspaper the three of us had created as co-editors.

After four editions of the weekly paper had miraculously been run off our Xerox machine and distributed to the camp, I began to believe that my therapeutic exercise in journalism had cured them sufficiently to function without alcohol in the real world outside our gates. It was Peckinpaugh's policy to get younger men (men in their thirties and forties) like these into jobs as quickly as possible. Employment proved the Camp's rehabilitation efforts successful, which meant bigger budget allotments from the city, and, like any good bureaucracy, success got measured in numbers on paper, not in flesh and blood and bone, in quantifiable increments rather than quality of life. I had seen this same scam in Vietnam with daily body counts. On paper, we seemed to be killing more Viet Cong than could possibly have existed. But, they just kept coming.

It was mid-morning in July. I walked across the sprawling campus and up the steps of the admin building. The cicadas rubbed their wings together and the electrical hum of summer rang in my ears. Allende, the recently democratically elected president of Chile had just been assassinated by Pinoche's right wing butchers, and Rosemarie's radio blared the story across the hallway as I entered my boss's office. That the coup had been backed by the Nixon government was obvious because the reporter kept repeating that the CIA had nothing to do with it. When the CIA denied something, it was a sure sign they were responsible, especially during this administration of solipsism that survived on misinformation and the undying illusion that a murderous rightwing dictator who was willing to allow U.S. corporations access to his country's natural resources was a much better ruler than a liberal socialist who questioned our capitalistic, elitist agenda.

Peckinpaugh rose from his desk and poured a cup of coffee, then returned to a stack of papers as if I didn't exist. Without raising his head, he said, "Isn't it about time to send the professor out on a job?"

"It's summer. There's no college looking for teachers right now."

"Oh God. You don't really believe a college would hire him, do you? Some of the summer resort camps in the Borsht Belt are looking for kitchen help."

"What would he be doing?"

"Washing the lettuce for salads and sweeping floors."

"The man held one of the most prestigious jobs in the academy. There's no way he can survive washing lettuce with Mexican migrants for minimum wage."

"Listen McGarrah, we can't cure these men. The best we can do is dry them out and hope they can become somewhat functional again.

I've got a new bus load of clients coming from the city and I need the beds. We can't coddle the ones that have the ability to work under their own steam. I've got a good deal with some of these resorts. We supply a lot of their labor for the summer…"

"…at a very low cost," I replied.

"…at a fair wage for services rendered. Get him packed. Besides, he'll be back in a week or two anyway."

"I don't think so. I've done him a lot of good down in the train station working on the newspaper. He feels like a whole man again. I'm sure he'll be fine."

"That's why I like you youngsters so much. Everything is simple. You pay the cab fare when he returns. It'll help remind you that life is more complex after you turn thirty."

At first, the professor seemed hesitant to leave his hairdresser friend. He blanched and balked and I thought he might have a seizure until I told him he would have his own room at the resort and a weekly paycheck that no one would take away from him. Then, he calmed down, threw his few belongings into a duffel bag, and I drove him to the bus station in Chester. From there, he disappeared into the Catskill Mountains.

For a week, his friend Ralph refused to give any of the other men at the camp haircuts. Pouting in his corner, he drank sugar-laden coffee constantly and rolled dozens of cigarettes every day, which he simply counted and stacked unsmoked in a shoebox. The newspaper press squealed to a halt.

Exactly seven days, or one pay period, from the professor's departure a taxi pulled up in front of the train station and deposited my rehabilitation effort on the cinder path without his duffel bag. His shirt was ripped to shreds, his jeans were soiled and stank of urine, and his left eye was black and blue. Two teeth had been knocked from his mouth, leaving a dark cavern between swollen lips. Ralph rushed to meet him. Throwing his arms around the professor's bruised shoulders, Ralph kissed him gently on his florid cheeks. Hand in hand they approached me. I could still smell the cheap, sweet wine on the brilliant man's breath.

"You people will never understand," said Ralph. "Pay the taxi driver."

"Understand what?" I answered, reaching in my pocket.

"Our kind can't function in a world of ignorance."

"The whole world's ignorant of one thing or another."

"But not of sexual preferences." The professor hissed the words out of the space where his teeth had been. "Here I was yesterday with my first pocketful of money in years. What was I supposed to do? I bought a bottle of good Canadian whiskey and invited Miguel, who I was washing lettuce with, back to my room for a drink. Now Ralph, explain to Master Jim what I like to do after a few drinks."

Ralph giggled and with slender fingers caressed the back of the professor's neck. "Well sweetie, you just love to fill your mouth with the taste of a real man."

"I think I get the picture. Your friend didn't appreciate your advances."

"Precisely. Not only that, but after he beat me up he stole my money. I didn't mind getting smacked around, but I did mind getting all my money stolen. Of course, that latent queen who runs the resort then had to fire me instead of Miguel or all his illegals would have quit. It simply isn't fair."

"It simply isn't fair," echoed Ralph.

The two men returned to their corner table in my makeshift rehab center. The Camp LaGuardia Weekly News returned to the makeshift press and my makeshift life went forward as before. Of course, this episode with the professor bolstered Peckinpaugh's long-standing opinion about the men he claimed were unworthy and incapable of rehabilitation, a fact he reminded me of a few days later when I came to his office begging relief from bugs.

"Real bugs," he said, "or bugs your boys have imagined."

"The place is full of roaches. No one should have to spend all day competing with roaches for space to sit or sugar to put in coffee."

"These inmates are living in paradise. Compared to where they came from, a building full of roaches is a huge step up. But I understand your need to coddle them."

In his defense, the director did send some bug spray my way. However, the roaches always returned, just as the men I sent forth to work did. Eventually, the roach situation and my continual complaints led to a bureaucratic nightmare with the main office in New York City, which caused me more problems with Peckinpaugh.

During those months at Camp LaGuardia, I never thought critically about the professor's behavior or related it to my own. Instead, I sat for hours on the huge paisley couch in my home outside of Chester and stared at the blank white sheetrock on the opposite wall. One of my friends named Spyder practiced the only song he knew on his Epiphone acoustic guitar *–come down off your throne and leave your body alone...and I can't find my way home* – and I felt myself dying, repeatedly. I waited, sometimes days and through many unbelievably bad renditions of the Blind Faith song, for the death I carried inside me from Vietnam to seep out my pores and wrap me in its protective cocoon, away from all the humanity I felt unfit to live with.

I empathized with the professor during these isolated moments, but I was decades away from realizing my memories of war had created similar feelings of unworthiness in me and put me on a similar path toward self-destruction. The chemicals I took when I first came back to escape my own thoughts, the inability to work out details in a complex relationship, the lack of desire to finish anything I started, the nightmares when I slept, the adrenalin bursts that shot through my veins as if those veins were detonation chord burning me from the inside out until the fire reached my mind and it exploded, none of these things registered as more than normal behavior for the confused society I was part of. At the time, even my increasing willingness to reach for whiskey rather than drugs seemed to be nothing more than finally becoming an adult rather than another way to self-medicate my pain.

Surviving my memories, both good and bad, has been a constant struggle for the last forty years, and I suspect a lot of people grapple with a similar issue. It has to do with nature more than nurture, I think. To overcome *self* and the negative proclivities that the self is heir to, a conscious desire to maintain worthiness is required.

The first step for me has been to clearly understand what is meant by the term and secondly to gauge if and how that definition might apply in each situation. A way I have come to consider the word worthy is to replace it with like words. Having value or merit, being useful and honorable, these are all ways I think about the word worthy when analyzing the direction of my life, where it's been, where it is, where it's going.

Believing that I'm the kind of person who chose the valuable and honorable course of action on those rare occasions when I did because I wanted to, because I was worthy, because it was an inherent part of who I happened to be, and not because it was the expedient course to take, is another matter entirely.

I'm not a psychologist and I'm not as smart as I sometimes pretend to be. Consequently, I don't understand all of the complexities involved in cultivating or losing the feeling of being worthy to walk in company with other humans. All I know is that the impression comes and goes these days more through vicarious interaction with peers or images of past transgressions than through tangible activity. Often, a downward slide begins with rejection by people I work beside who have earned my respect or admiration. But just as often it's generated by a memory that claws its way to my consciousness from some deep subconscious hole where it was buried years before.

I don't mean guilt. Guilt is a different wound entirely and one I rarely open anymore, having resigned myself years ago to the fact that all of us are flawed and make mistakes that we have little, if any, control over. This emotion is deeper, more visceral. It rises from an inability to accept my own uniqueness, a willingness to allow society the power to judge my humanity and a weakness to agree with that assessment even when it denies good things I know to be true about myself.

The professor taught me a lesson that's taken me a lifetime to learn, a lesson he never learned. Relativity grows in leaps and bounds from the soil in what the word worthy is planted. Worthiness can relate to the way you do a job, conduct yourself in a restaurant, get offered a scholarship, raise a child, vote, what church you attend, what race you belong to, what social group you associate with, where you buy a home, where you shop for clothes, whether you believe in global warming, whether you don't believe in global warming, and this list could continue for several more pages. However, the word *worthy* describes a quality arising from how you perceive the value of any and all of these things when spread over your life.

During the periods in which I allowed others to dictate my status in the human race based on their values alone, most often my life failed like the professor's did. On the other hand, when balancing outside opinions with my own perspectives and permitting myself the last definition of my own worth, my subsequent actions have led to a temporary sort of inner peace, and that's resulted in some positive contributions to family, neighborhood, and society, efforts that are tangible and quantifiable.

I didn't relate this event as a sermon. It is neither a morality play, nor a chapter in a best-selling "chicken soup for low esteem" kind of self-help book. I simply wanted to relate a story about one old drunk and how an encounter with him may have pulled me back from the edge of an abyss I teetered on after returning from war. But as with most real narratives, I suspect there are a lot of men and women who, for a lot of different reasons, have grappled with the same concept of being worthy. Some of them may read this story and take it in an entirely different way than I intended.

If you happen to be one of those people, please feel free to judge whether that reading was worthy use of your time and energy. Your opinion won't change the fact that writing it was certainly worthy of mine.

My America

1.*The Man in the Street*

Not long ago, I went grocery shopping, not an unusual event for a serious eater like myself. I like to go anytime I feel a sense of urgency for food because it takes me about one-tenth of the time to go through the same list as my wife. Anyway, here I am coming out of the Kroger's store on a well-travelled, busy street in Louisville, Kentucky, when I see a man standing in the middle of the road straddling the white line as cars whizzed by him on both sides. He seemed to be staring at the blue tongues on his dirty and worn sneakers. There were no laces in those shoes. The grey coat he wore hung in taters off his thin frame. He stood on legs more like bicycle spokes than flesh and bones. His unshaven face looked the same color as the coat, and he puffed at the remnant of a cigarette. When he took the butt out of his mouth, the man stared at the ash as if it were sculpted by Rodin and dropped it on the pavement. His feet never moved at all and acknowledged nothing, neither horns blowing nor drivers cursing. I suspected he was homeless but could have been a prophet as well.

2.*Hometown Buffet*

I was hungry after struggling in a classroom with a group of college freshmen all morning. As I contemplated my wonder at how difficult it was to teach the basic concepts of being human, or even create an interest in the importance of Humanities to education, I turned into the parking lot of an American phenomenon, the all-you-can-eat for one price, take-what-you-want, but please-eat-all-you-take restaurant. This type of dining proliferated in the Midwest and the South in the late 20th century.

Buffet eating was an upgrade of old-style cafeteria dining. You remember what I'm talking about, the place that your parents took you after church on Sundays where you select a plastic tray from a stack of them, place the tray on a metal rail attached to a steam table full of various slop, and slide it toward a cashier. Behind a glass plate along that rail minimum-wage workers stand in a row behind the metal bins of slop being warmed by the steam table. The servers spoon individual portions on a plate as you choose them and move down the line. The cashier looks at your plate and adds up your bill on a register. This modern iteration removes the workers and the glass partition between customers and slop. You scoop your own having paid one price before you start at the back of the line. You eat and return to the steam table as often as you like and take what you want. When supplies get low, a single worker comes from the kitchen with a fresh bucket of slop for the steam table. It's the miracle of Capitalism. Low overhead and minimum employees for management, low quality product and indigestion for the greedy customer.

That was a digression in my point, but a necessary explanation for readers unfamiliar with the American economy. But now you know the type of eatery I had chosen for my lunch, and I wasn't alone. The place filled with hungry people rapidly. I filled two plates with ham, green beans, macaroni and fried chicken along with various pies and cakes for dessert. By the way, I'm fat.

As I searched for a seat like a lost child, an elderly stranger, a white-haired lady, waved at me and pointed to an empty chair at her table for two.

"I just hate eating alone," she said as I slid into the chair across from hers.

We did not introduce ourselves and exchanged the bare minimum of pleasantries between bites. When I finished, I thanked her for the company and rose to leave. I struggled with my coat as I had injured my left shoulder playing tennis the day before. The lady noticed my discomfort jumped up from her seat, lifted the side of my coat guiding my arm into the sleeve. The act was a minor one and not usually worth as much attention as I'm giving it. But it reminded me in a major way that most people are kind, even to strangers, if given the opportunity. I forget that fact often in this fast-paced, stressful, self-serving world we live in, and I try to remember my responsibility to be kind myself when I think of the incident. Kindness is not an inherent quality in America. It is a learned discipline and worth cultivating.

3.*Three-card Monty:*

Politics in America is a con game of Three-card Monty. We've all seen it played either in some back alley or on TV. You put your money down, and the dealer shows you an ace, places it face down on a table with two other cards. He shuffles the three cards in and out, round and round with rapid twists of his wrists until he's satisfied you are sufficiently confused. Then, he says with a smirk, "Which one is the ace?" You pick and guess what? You lose. He turns one of the other cards over and up comes the ace. You're convinced that the game is fair, and you just barely missed choosing the right card. You'll cash in big time very soon. Down goes the money again and again and again. You place it on the table until you're broke, and you have no idea how that could happen. The next payday you play some more to recoup what you lost. The game is about power and control. The dealer has the power to manipulate you so you feel like you're going to win, but he has control over the ace so you never do. In American politics, it's much the same. Through the shuffling of media stories and the promise of a winning ace, each political party creates a feeling in its voters that if you choose their candidates you will profit by your choice. Somehow, it never happens. Only the dealers win.

4. *Labor Day Never Stops for Some*

It is 1912. Sophie begins her workday at 4am, seven days a week. Standing on a mound of empty sharp shells so she can reach into a narrow wooden trough piled high with live oysters, she nods to the girls on each side. They barely acknowledge her presence. Each girl stretches her arms into the pile, grasps an oyster shell with one hand and inserts a metal shucking tool in a ligament between the shell halves called the umbo with the other. The umbo holds the shell together tightly. With a violent twist the girls pry the halves open, forcing the mystical-sounding muscle into exposing the soft-bodied oyster inside. The oyster, still alive, is severed with a twist of the blade and shucked into a pot at the foot of each worker, and the shells are tossed with the clinking sound of breaking glass into the pile that grows ever higher on the dirt floor.

By noon, Sophie's hands bleed from fondling the shells as if from a hundred tiny razor cuts. Eventually, in days or weeks, the shells on the floor will slice the thin soles of her only shoes, and from that day forward, she will go home in the evening with her feet bleeding like her hands until she can afford to patch her shoes. During the summer, the huge warehouse on the Alabama dock where the oysters are brought in swelters as a single fan barely moves the heavy air enough for her to breathe. During winter, a small wooden stove will warm her body when she is allowed close to it once every few hours. Sophie is white yet speaks no English to ask for a doctor even if one were available. Her injuries and illnesses remain without remedy unless some folk treatment is applied at home. At sundown her work for the day will stop, and if she has filled at least six pots full of shucked oysters, a foreman will pay her thirty cents that she will take home to help the family survive.

The girl came to America from some small country in central Europe with her parents seeking a better life. She never learns to read or write and dies when most of us begin to really live. Sophie is the oldest of the group. She is ten, and this is life from beginning to end.

It is 2012. We are a civilized nation now. Machines shuck and can our oysters. You rarely see us white folk working with primitive tools anymore, unless it's in our gardens pruning the roses. Small family farms are still difficult to manage. But they are few and far between, having been bought out and replaced by huge mechanized corporate farms.

Many factories have been partially or fully robotized and require only a handful of operators. The fast-food franchises employ a mostly younger workforce part time. All employers are governed by strict child labor laws and OSHA. Some even provide benefits. Some help pay tuition for education. However, we still and always will have food and lifestyle products that must be handled by a tactile work force. For example, machines don't pick all the strawberries, especially on huge corporate farms. People do. The same thing is true for oranges, apples, sweet potatoes, and a host of other produce and products that go from field to market. Most of the workers are immigrants, many illegal, who have paid exorbitant fees to be smuggled here with the hope of living better. Maybe they do live better, maybe they don't. Most are no longer from Central Europe, but rather from South America, and they work for pennies on the dollar until caught or forced to move on. When we celebrate the Labor Day holiday, do we really celebrate for all workers.

5.*Free Market Enterprise*

Not long ago, I bought a new pair of sneakers for hiking. At my age, the chance of wearing out a pair of sneakers from hiking anywhere is limited, but occasionally, I just get tired of looking at the old ones. These were made by a company called Skechers, but they got my thinking about the first pair I wore, which was in 1956—Converse high-tops. Converse were American made. The company originated in 1908, building a factory in a town named Malden in the state of Massachusetts. In 2001, Converse went bankrupt, and the name brand was bought by Nike. Now, every Converse pair you buy are really Nike shoes in disguise.

This isn't unusual. Corporations swallow up brands all the time and sell products with familiar names. Americans have confidence that those products will be as usable as the brand implies. Sometimes it is, sometimes it is not. I think that Converse sneakers are probably still well made, albeit for a much bigger price and a much wider profit margin that in 1956 when mine carried me up and down the length of a basketball floor as an eight-year-old.

Of course, this is all nostalgic memory that creeps into an old man's mind on occasion, but before I lose track of my point in memory and drift away, let me get to that point. There was a lot of controversy when Converse in 2001 got in bed with Nike because of Nike's business practices. I was in the process of writing a magazine essay that I never finished on their ethics. The subject piqued my interest because of Vietnam, especially as a veteran of the Vietnam war.

Nike had built an ultra-modern factory in that country a few years earlier and, as it turned out, many of their sporting equipment line was being made there, as well as across other countries in Southeast Asia. It seems that their sweaty equipment, footballs, sneakers, and jerseys were produced in sweat shops while being sold for a tremendous markup to American consumers. Vietnamese women labored making sneakers for twenty cents an hour and if production fell, those women were subjected to corporal punishment. At the same time, footballs were being stitched by children in Pakistan who were paid sixty cents a day.

When the horrendous working conditions and pay got discovered by the American news media, the public began to raise objections. Nike sales plummeted momentarily and so did their profits. Yes, it was an outrage. We demanded conditions change. The company apologized profusely on the news and in commercials. Notice the word, momentarily. The Nike ad campaign continued with professional athletes, particularly basketball players, stoking the desire for Nike products. Notice a little irony here. The starting pay twenty years ago when I researched this article, the minimum fucking wage for the NBA, was 247,500 dollars a year. As my old man use to quip, "money talks and bullshit walks." The Nike ad campaign worked, and very shortly, stock dividends soared once again. Twenty years later their products still fly off the shelves. Today, the average MSRP of Nike shoes is $110.15 while the average available lowest price is $66.75. The average US adult labors for 9.79 hours at work in order to afford each pair of Nike shoes that they buy. The market remains free—for some—not so much for others.

6. *Genetics*

My father loved horse racing. Nothing gave him a bigger thrill than a day at Churchill Downs or Keeneland or Ellis Park. The scent of horse liniment wafted through the air as a line of horses pranced into the paddock for saddling before each race hypnotized him. Add that to a beer in one hand the Racing Form in the other, the whispers of expectation erupting from the crowd into a roar as the thoroughbreds bolted away from the clanging bell when the starting gates flew open, and his day was filled with joy. When he lost money, he never complained. When he won, he never bragged. Gambling didn't drive him to the track as much as the science of breeding and the notion of its importance.

Breeding is one major factor when translated into a term horse racing experts call "Class" or sometimes "Heart" as a synonym. Theoretically, the better bred a horse is the more competitive it will be in a race and the more value it has. It is an almost mystical term that rises above athletic ability. For example, if I were to put two horses in a race and all other things being equal, including their speed, the horse with the best bloodlines would theoretically end up finishing first most of the time. At its most basic level, we're talking about equine eugenics.

Eugenics developed as the study of how to arrange reproduction within a human population to increase the occurrence of heritable characteristics regarded as desirable. While it may prove valuable to study horse breeding, it has proved unscientific and disastrous among humans. Think of how the Nazis perverted it to murder eight million Jews. Think of how Americans used it to enslave blacks and slaughter Native Americans. It simply does not work when a species has free will to make choices that perpetuate "class" and "heart" by race and color or when circumstances intervene at random to alter completely a person's environment and lifestyle. Or so I thought at one time in my life. I have some personal knowledge of what I thought to be this reality.

On the other hand, my daughter researches our heritage by examining DNA and ancestral lineage. This has led me to believe that genetics also plays a major role, not in creating random circumstances, but in circumstances we create with our own behavior and how we respond to both random and self-generated circumstances. Recently she discovered that through my grandmother's line on my father's side of the family we are descended from a Scottish lord and his wife, who was herself a notorious witch back in the day. Piecing this together with my cousin Rosemary's research, which concludes we came from a line of whisky-riddled Irish Presbyterian ministers through my grandfather's line on my father's side. I was able to establish a basis for my noble arrogance that tends to rear its drunken head when bourbon becomes available.

What shocked me most came from my daughter's discovery that through DNA analysis of my mother's side of the family, I could boast of royal—as in monarchial—ancestors as well. It turns out I was descended from Marie Antoinette. Parsing this bit of information led me to understand why I'm overweight and seem to have no discipline when it comes to shedding my excess pounds. I've inherited a problem from cousin Marie. I'm cursed with a love of cake. It isn't my fault. There is now scientific proof available that I will eat almost any kind of cake almost anyone will bake, and as much as possible.

This fact doesn't make me worthy of getting my head cut off, necessarily. It does, however, answer some of my personal questions about why I seem to give myself over to excessive behavior at times. I am royalty and entitled to do whatever I want. For example, I will eat two Big Macs if they are available, watch the same movie over and over if it fills some adventurous or romantic delusion in my life, and a half-empty bottle of bourbon is unbearable to me. There is no such thing as a "small" risk for me, which explains over a dozen broken bones and four marriages. I like tobacco and am quite capable on a mountain top of pissing into the wind. Many careers have begun and ended during my youth—warrior, teacher, horse trainer, mail carrier, evangelist, construction foreman, carpet layer, bartender, social worker, and car salesman, to name a few. I have managed to live a relatively happy life and raise a couple of great children. While most of my failures have found excuses in my proclivities for extreme behavior, I have found an excuse for my extreme behavior. I was born this way. I can't help it. Right now at the age of 76, I am a firm believer in equality, compassion, charity, peace, and freedom. So, I'm thinking of going to a Trump rally where I live here in the deep South wearing a *Vote for Anybody but Trump* tee shirt. It's in my genes to make people angry. What could go wrong?

7. *The Celebration of War*

I belong to a group that claims to expose the "true" cost of war by recording statistics on bookmarkers and mailing those small pieces of paper to possible contributors. That's a good thing, I suppose, noting the millions turned into corpses at random and reminding us some humans have killed for pleasure, greed, religion, and racial hatred, calling it duty or honor or patriotism through most of our history. But, dogs don't breed cats. So, I don't see how nameless numbers give birth to remorse, even though Veterans for Peace is a tireless promoter for a saner world in every format imaginable.

A famous French writer in the 19th century named de Maupassant once said that humans have two choices. We can be happy or we can have knowledge, but to maintain both is not possible. The more we learn, especially about human nature, the less blissful our sojourn among our fellow beasts becomes. Why? Because we are able to see both good and evil qualities that reside in us all and, if we are blessed with any semblance of conscience, at some point the evil becomes inexcusable. It will not disappear from our minds simply by chanting any one of many clichéd mantras such as "god is on our side" or "mission accomplished." Blind credulity will no longer suffice once we are aware of our own unlimited capacity for cruelty. Knowledge of reality always overshadows wishful thinking. This is especially true of soldiers and civilians overwhelmed by war.

The true cost of war is measured by intimate knowledge of blood and fire, lifting seared flesh and unattached limbs from the broken rubble of homes and schools, digging graves for mothers and babies still warm in the womb. The true cost of war is quantified not by death or money only but through the misery of its living participants after the fact – the emotional turmoil, the survivor's guilt, the grief, the nightmares, the pathological dysfunction of homeless veterans, the missing arms and legs, the vacant souls. The families of veterans often end up broken as well, expecting their returned hero to be the same man or woman who left them for war.

The evil in humans that allows them to start new wars isn't born from those who have knowledge of its consequences, or care much about those consequences. Wars are not started by soldiers. They begin with politicians, most of whom have never made nor ever will make Guy de Maupassant's choice between knowledge and happiness. These are the cowards who kill for the reasons I stated earlier, the ones that never get blood on their hands, the ones that never see the faces of the dead in their dreams. They maintain their joy through the ignorance of their arrogance. Consider the meaningless invasion of Iraq and the tens of thousands, American and Iraqi, that died because of it. Don't get me wrong. I'm not a pacifist. I'm glad Osama bin Laden caught a bullet in the brain pan. He earned it. I would have done it myself, gladly. I've done worse things as a soldier. But, I am a conscientious objector. I object through my sense of morality and ethical integrity to the reasons certain leaders use their militaries for personal agendas and to the misery that causes.

I feel saddened that my father spent his youth fighting Hitler in Europe and Africa, but I understand the necessity of doing it. On the other hand, when I look back on my own experiences as a Marine in Vietnam a different understanding emerges. America engaged in what historians now call "flexible" warfare, which simply means a modern policy of sending our young men and women into harm's way with no long-term goals or with unattainable ones and with end results that only serve a very small section of our citizenry. Publicly, Vietnam was a war to stop the spread of Russian communism. Privately and politically, it was a war to control the strategic and economic resources of a small third world country for the benefit of American corporations. Russian communism was never exported to Vietnam and what exists there today is an amalgamation of several political philosophies, including a type of totalitarian governmental capitalism supported by our government. Don't take my word for what I'm writing here. Do your own research. These facts are available. It just takes some effort.

In the 21st century, flexible warfare has morphed into preemptive warfare, meaning our politicians give themselves the moral exigency to start these flexible and limited actions by establishing a just cause for them through propaganda beforehand. In other words, *we need to be the aggressor against them before (substitute any country we desire to invade) they become the aggressor toward us.* Remember the nonexistent "weapons of mass destruction?" This is especially true when our politicians own stock in military/industrial corporations (for example, Cheney and Halliburton) that can be offered no-bid contracts and given huge profits for killing, or when oil companies that donate millions to political campaigns (for example, the four Bush campaigns – senior and junior) need their reserves protected so their corporate stocks maintain high value.

I'm a storyteller by trade and by spirit. Let me tell you a story. I have a very close friend, a good man, a family man, an intelligent man who paid a dear cost for his service to his country. As a matter of fact, he is paying still. My friend played football at our high school and played very well. I believe he might have gone on to some serious university team if he had been blessed with no conscience. But we were all from southern Indiana, a place where god was good in 1968, and commies were the spawn of Satan. They hid under every rock. They lurked in every shadow. Like many of us, my friend watched a lot of John Wayne movies and from them developed a celluloid sense of duty. By that, I mean he built an emotional construct based on Hollywood rather than reality. Good guys wear white hats. Good guys – meaning patriotic, conservative, Nixonian Republican, white Christians – always won. Good guys never died; they just rode off into the sunset with a beautiful submissive woman draped across the saddle.

Believing what he had been taught from infancy forward, my friend fulfilled his responsibility and enlisted in the army. He became an outstanding helicopter pilot in Vietnam, a treetop flyer, skimming over the jungle and bravely out maneuvering the .50 caliber machine guns of the Viet Cong. He had one job, carrying young boys into battle and ferrying their torn, lifeless bodies from the battlefield back to some rear area morgue. Oh sorry, two jobs. Then, he had to flush the blood out of his helicopter with a water hose. Week after week, month after month, his life evolved into days of loading and unloading dead boys and nights of drinking whiskey to forget the days. He never got wounded. He never killed anybody. He simply stacked up men who were already dead like he threw hay bales into the barn loft on those southern Indiana summer days between semesters of high school.

When he came home, he did what the rest of us did, went back to college or got a job or got married and started a beautiful family. Most of that went on during the day. His nights were given over to the dead, and he went back to the one thing that buried the dead for him in Vietnam, alcohol. Years went by; bottle after bottle was drained dry and still the dead refused to stay buried. Post Traumatic Stress Disorder didn't exist anywhere in the 1970's except in the minds of Vietnam veterans. The government refused to acknowledge it and the VA doctors blamed the nightmares, the rage, the substance abuse and fear of intimacy, the inability to focus, the clinical depression and flashbacks on other *non-military* causes. It was cheaper that way. My friend didn't have a problem with his memories of war, not really. He simply couldn't handle the stresses of his job and his marriage. Shit happens, right?

Eventually, he drank enough vodka and scotch that leaving for work in the morning was no guarantee for his family that he would return home in the evening. Sometimes, he stopped for a quick cocktail and woke up in a different town three or four days later with no knowledge of where he was or how he got there. Then his liver began to fail. This probably saved his life. By the time he ended up in the VA hospital, various government bureaucrats and medical people had begun to admit that maybe, just maybe, war might create residual problems for those who lived through it. Maybe the mind wasn't meant to look at what extreme violence forced it to see.

During the Clinton presidency, the Veterans Administration underwent radical change and became an efficient and professional health delivery system for both physical and mental problems. It was a good thing because we had recently ended another one of those flexible wars in the Middle East called Desert Storm. A lot of us, including my friend, took advantage of what we were finally being offered and our lives began to change for the better. In 1997, I went back to college and found my friend already enrolled. Having been sober for eight years, he was ready to tackle a university education.

I was lucky. Something in my brain clicked around all those books and I took flight in my mind. In two years, I received a BA degree, and in two more years, I completed two graduate programs and began writing books and teaching. My friend – not so much. He was, he is, smarter than me and in many ways a better person than me. But his PTSD will not allow him to finish anything he starts. I don't know why. No one can answer that, no doctors or preachers or even my friend. He only knows that he will sit in a classroom and make A's till the last couple of weeks of the semester and then withdraw from the class. It isn't a matter of work interfering because he isn't able to work a steady job. Perhaps living through the war while so many young men didn't generated an overwhelming sense of guilt. Why does he deserve happiness and success? What makes him any better than all those bodies he still carries in his mind? This is called *survivor's guilt* and it's part of the cost combat veterans who continue to live must continue to pay.

I haven't seen my buddy in over five years, but the last time I saw him I was in his town signing copies of a new book. I met him at a bar. Yes, he was drinking again but assured me only an occasional cocktail before dinner and maybe just one or two after. Everything was under control. The kids had survived adolescence and gone to various colleges to form lives of their own. Now that he could rattle around an empty house, putter in the garden, and read books, without interruption, he felt well enough in his mind to handle drinking again. This is what he said, but both of us knew the truth. In the absence of the daily chaos involved with raising children and working for a living, the dead were beginning to seep back into his consciousness, resurrected by loneliness.

Don't get me wrong. This seems like a very sad story, but it has good elements in it. My friend is a survivor. Like the rest of us, he's happy to be breathing. He has a beautiful wife, great kids, and like me, he's had forty plus years that many young men in our generation never had. I'm not asking you to feel sorry for him. We're talking about the true cost of war, and I want you to know that it's more than the immediate dead, more than billions of dollars of destruction, more than great Diasporas. Although, all those things are incredibly important. The true cost also involves your neighbors, normal men and women, trying to live productive lives, people struggling with the same difficult problems you are and one more – the memory of carnage and smoke and fire – that influences every waking minute of their lives.

When you check your Memorial Day list for charcoal and steaks, beer and ice, sun block and apple pie, take a minute to think about why you are free to enjoy those things. When you ask yourself "Did I remember everything," remember that the United States is involved in three flexible wars right now, and we won't understand the "true" cost of these wars for at least a generation. Right now, the military is dealing with the highest suicide rate in its history, and this doesn't include the deaths from drug overdoses, motorcycle accidents, and other forms of risky behavior that recently discharged combat veterans carry out. We have no idea of the amount of death and destruction or its cost in the countries where we wage these wars. We may never understand that completely. I have lost friends and comrades who died forty years after the fact from Agent Orange exposure or other wounds incurred in Vietnam. Forty years from now, veterans of Iraq and Afghanistan will be dying of similar health problems.

Today, Congress whines and cries about debt reduction and getting our budget under control. They fight over what programs to dismantle and who must make the economic sacrifices. However, I hear no serious debate on cutting defense contracts, no arguments about eliminating weapons the military doesn't want or even need because those weapons are built by some senator's constituents. There are no ongoing peace discussions with any hope of honest resolution. War is good business, and the cost of war is never borne by the politicians who authorize it or the corporations that profit from it. The only way the true cost of war will ever get disclosed in its entirety is if most citizens not directly struggling with that cost in some direct way demand a share in it. So far, this has never happened. Consequently, we go on paying the price through the sacrifice of a small segment of our population, most often the young and bright. It's easy to bear the cost of war when we have the luxury of choosing not to know or remember the dead and the wounded. But for veterans, the dead never die and the living are often unable to get on with their lives. Please, as you enjoy this Memorial Day, take a minute to contemplate how much your gasoline is *really* costing.

9. *Idle Thoughts That Were Worth Thinking:*

There are whole days in Indiana that break the landscape of winter like a small oasis interrupts the endless sand of a desert with mercy, kindness, anticipation, and joy. The sun is high and bright, almost white and warm that will invigorate a few small, random carpet-like squares of green grass growing on the dead ground. People move thoughtfully from place to place as if to taste the air and ruminate on it slowly like a piece of cotton candy. The taste makes them smile, disappears and returns with every step. You can imagine a future spring day sitting on the bank of a small pond and tossing out a line. Even if no bluegill or catfish are biting, the thrill of not having to function like a nine to five automaton is possible, the image brings you comfort, and life is worth your time.

10. *While Drinking Scotch One Night*

A.

I was watching an old movie made from an older novel recently called *The Last Temptation of Christ*. The last temptation, of course, had to be sex with Mary Magdeline. In movies and books written within the Judeo/Christian tradition sex is always a temptation, never a pleasure or a lucky break, but rather a tortured excursion into Satanville with the engine misfiring due to the corrosive wear and tear of guilt. But I digress. During the movie, I realized, or maybe reaffirmed is a better term, my strong objection to organized religion. The problem, especially with the Christian religion, is not what was originally taught by teachers before their thoughts were turned into organized religion. Siddhârtha Gautama was not a Buddhist. He was a teacher who taught a way of life, a path to walk. Jesus was not a Christian. He was a Jew who had profound insight into human nature and taught us how to live with each other in peace. The problem lies with the application of what these men preached by the mysterious members of esoteric priesthoods who have their own agendas, and, for most, those agendas directly correspond with their own perpetuation in an exclusive lifestyle. Beyond that, a matter of priorities takes over.

Most denominations of the Christian religion, for example, fixate on certain doctrines peculiar to the beliefs of their founders and then claim that *his* original *leader* was Jesus Christ, using some statement, or interpretation of some statement, from Jesus to support their claim. For example, there are sects that claim alcohol is forbidden, dancing is forbidden, blood transfusions are forbidden. Others claim homosexuals are going to hell along with Muslims, Jews, Hindus, and Buddhists, as well as any Baptist, Catholic, Methodist, Presbyterian, or Pentecostal that doesn't accept the slant on the scriptures that built their group. The point I'm making here is simple. This need for material growth and expansion within each of these organizations causes the establishment of doctrines and dogmas that encourage the expansion. This, in turn, causes the most fundamental and important and universal of Jesus' teachings to be pushed aside or forgotten entirely, namely *LOVE*. He wasn't kidding when he said the most important commandment from any god is to love our neighbors as we love ourselves and he didn't rhetorically define neighbors. The word was all-inclusive. Till we arrive at the point that we can understand and apply this most simple, yet most profound, of all *human* teachings, we don't have much chance for a peaceful and morally productive world.

B.

The first ancient members of my family seem to have originated somewhere in the Scottish Highlands. Like peering through a fog in the early dawn, only vague suggestions and inferences can be drawn to assume what you think you see is accurate in that regard. All that is known for sure is the fact that Celtic blood runs through my veins if you believe DNA testing and the fact that I get goosebumps when I hear bagpipes. Recorded history provides more clarity. Several hundred years ago the name McGarragh—now spelled McGarrah—appears on a list of Celt families that settled in Ireland, County Sligo to be precise and remained there until part of a diaspora to the New World in the early 18th century. (i.e. this knowledge made available through the genealogical research of my cousin Rosemary McGarrah).

Throw one of the labels Scottish or Irish or Scotch-Irish at me and it will stick. I'm not claiming any bragging rights about my heritage. I am thoroughly American several generations past being any kind of immigrant. Nevertheless, I have always felt a bond that goes beyond drinking green beer on St. Patrick's Day or a desire to watch the movie *Braveheart* more than once. So, imagine my delight yesterday when I discovered a way to become part of the landed gentry in Scotland and get drunk at the same time.

The opportunity presented itself through the purchase of one bottle of Laphroaig single malt scotch. Laphroaig is a Gaelic word untranslatable into English that might mean "beautiful hollow by the broad bay," or possibly "beautiful broad by the hollow bay" depending on how much scotch you drink. Anyway, by virtue of the whisky, I became a friend of Laphroaig Distillery and was allowed to claim a plot of land in this beautiful hollow by the broad bay. All I had to do was go to their website, enter a special code number, fill out a form, fill out the form again because I left information out, fill out the form again because I left different information out, drink two shots of the newly bought whisky, and fill out the form again.

Now, I am classed for all eternity as "A friend of Laphroaig" and will soon receive via the mail, which in America and thanks to Louis DeJoy can take months, a personalized certificate of ownership with my individual plot number for one square foot of Scottish land. Bonus: I will also be able to enter the Friends of Laphroaig website and receive redeemable gift shop points for every bottle I buy going forward.

Was it worth the fifty bucks and the effort? Well, I am proud to be an owner of ground that may or may not contain the blanched bones of my Celtic warrior ancestors. But the fifty bucks? I can't answer that till the bottle's empty.

C.

A Southern Freight train rumbled by on the tracks a block from my home. The whistle blew at the instant I began pouring my third Laphroaig scotch and caused me to spill an extra dram in my glass. I blessed the sound and at the same time remembered Jerry Miller. Jerry was a senior in high school and several years older than me when he became a local legend. Although, the fame he garnered must have felt hard-earned after-the-fact and not one to be casually repeated by aspiring romantics like me.

He came up with the bright idea of "hopping" one of the trains that passed routinely through our small Southern Indiana town. The trains left the sliding doors on empty cars and were obliged legally to slow down to a crawl as they passed through street intersections until they cleared the town limits and found themselves on open tracks. Not every engineer adhered to those limits, especially if the train was behind schedule. Added to this, the clackety-clack-clack of the metal wheels on metal tracks increased with just a slight upturn of speed. Anyone familiar with long freight trains and the sound they make will agree the repetition has a mesmerizing effect on someone standing near the tracks. Coupled with the warm breeze and the exotic scent of burnt deasil fuel, the call of adventure and the dream of faraway places was almost irresistible to a young adventurer who never had an adventure but had been raised on the mythological stories of Depression era hoboes as most of us were in those days of the early 1960's. I blame our grandparents for this.

No one ever accused Jerry of brilliance, and I believe the sound hypnotized him. He spotted an empty freight car and began sprinting beside it along the tracks. As it slowed, sort of, for an intersection, Jerry leapt toward the dark void inside the slightly opened sliding door. He wasn't going anywhere in particular. He just wanted to go somewhere. Grabbing for the ladder on the side of the empty grain car, his foot slipped from the bottom rung. A metal wheel rolled over Jerry's foot and crushed it. Half of the foot was amputated. I'm sure the pain seemed unbearable, and he hobbled around town for years after.

The moral of his encounter is obvious. Don't attempt to hop on moving trains. But we live in America, a land of opportunity and lawsuits.

We are taught from childhood that bad situations or circumstances will happen to us at some point in life. A good citizen must learn to make the best of them, even if we caused them. The thing I remember most about the hobbling Jerry did was that it carried him from wherever he happened to be to the driver's side door of his new Mercedes. Whether he would sacrifice the car for a new foot, I never asked him.

10. *Election Night*

On the first Tuesday of November every four years, many small rural towns in the Midwest conduct local elections. Sometimes elections coincide with national politics and sometimes they are independently held replacing town council members, school board officials, sheriffs, dog catchers, and various other candidates for jobs that pay less than they should but also require less time and effort as a career. What they bring to a farmer, the manager of a grocery store, an insurance salesman, or other ordinary people is more important in the community than money. It is status. Along with this feeling of importance comes a release from the banality of day-to-day living. Being elected by your neighbors, peers, and distant relatives, inflates your sense of self-worth without having to work too hard and, in most cases, gives you some power if you win your office without much stress over the petty responsibilities that office will control.

In my hometown this has always created an illusion of importance that far-outweighed the reality of it. Think of Christmas, New Year's, the county fair, and the Fourth of July all at once. If I described one of these nights from fifty years ago, it would be the same as one of these nights presently. The town square fills with people. There are always a couple of empty storefronts from closed-down, moved-out, can't-make-a-living local businesses that were replaced by a Walmart. One houses the local Democrat election committee and another, the Republican. The store fronts are strung with Christmas tree lights and old men huddle by the front door exchanging stories from past elections. Unattended children run screaming through the crowds gathered just outside.

Banners and ribbons unfurl behind some of them in the breeze and flap like tais on attention-deficit comets. You may try to park in the one space left open around either building only to be cursed by an old woman who stands in the space. She has been saving it for her husband's pickup truck. He is driving around the block. Someone usually runs a straw poll and keeps track of estimated tallies. They scratch the numbers with a bar of Ivory soap on the plate glass windows of their respective headquarters. Republicans usually find themselves ahead. No one in the crowd wants to admit voting for one of them there liberals.

The next morning, the streets are sweep clean, the shoe store, the jewelry shop, the bridal shop, the pool room, and two diners are open for business as usual, along with the courthouse. Administrations will have changed, maybe not. I knew a town that had the same Republican mayor for twenty-four years.

11. *The Perfect Sausage Sandwich*

If you had happened to be in Athens, Georgia, a few years ago on most any given weekend you may have been subjected to the most amazing of culinary delights without ever entering a restaurant, an important consideration in the time of a pandemic. But you would have wandered through various neighborhood intersections till you discovered the telltale scent of grilled onions and the sight of a light gray plume of smoke rising into the clouds to have found it. On a corner or in an empty parking lot a sign reads "Home of J.B. Sausages."

It's a simple place this home, a small trailer hitched and parked behind a battered pickup truck. A narrow smokestack rises from the black tin roof and connects under that roof to a fifty-five-gallon drum sawn if half, hinged, and converted into a makeshift cooking grill. Furnishings are sparse in the kingdom, a shelf for various condiments, including and especially two or three types of mustard, and a wooden bench opposite the grill where J.B. himself sits to stoke the coals beneath the sizzling onions, sautéed peppers, and plump, juicy, roasting meat.

The jolly man waits for customers rain or shine. They will come and willingly wait in line as if communion is offered and they respond to the invocation "Lord, I am not worthy, only feed me that sausage for six bucks and I shall be healed." Okay, that's hyperbolic. The experience isn't quite that intense and all you will be saved from temporarily is the empty feeling in your stomach.

Real Polish sausage is born from a mysterious mixture of eighty per cent pork, twenty percent beef, salt, pepper, sugar, garlic, and marjoram. The meat gets cured first, mixed with the spices, stuffed into a sausage casing, and then hot smoked. Everyone has a secret way of conjuring the unique taste of different brands. I don't know what J.B. does to his, but I'm convinced there is some supernatural force at work. When the first bite hits your taste buds it is possible to get a gastronomical rush that could be described by a hungry person as a light hit from a line of cocaine. Ultimately though, the overall experience cannot be explained by sausage or condiments alone.

There are other empty feelings besides a visceral appetite that may be satiated by stopping by for a visit. Make sure you have the time. While cooking a polish sausage on a red-hot grill isn't a long-term task, J.B. provides other services. For his fee of six dollars, you may get a conversation if you're lonely, a bit of therapy if you're in need, some comfort for recent anguish, a lesson in culinary art, or a bit of job counseling if you want to change careers. What each customer is sure to enjoy is the level of personal interaction often missing at a fast-food drive-thru or a busy diner. If patience is not your virtue, go somewhere else. J.B. doesn't care. He isn't feeding you so he'll get rich, at least not economically.

Post Script: October 29/ 2021—I have learned that J.B. is no longer in business. This sad development comes from the stunted and restrictive view of law an community statutes. We need rules to live in societies, granted. But we also need some common sense in the application of rules. For whatever reason, and there could be many self-serving ones involved, our philosophical vender has been run out of town. J.B., by virtue of an obscure ordinance, can no longer sell his polish sausages in Athens, Georgia. Evidently, his tiny operation was taking customers away from the local purveyors of poison fast-food fat, and their multimillion-dollar income was threatened by an old black man who mainly wanted company.

12. *Subways and Cynics*

Riding the subway between Times Square and Greenwich Village not so long ago, I noticed a man wearing a blue nylon jacket, red ball cap, and faded Levis. He carried a light blue knapsack. The man seemed to be Hispanic, but in this time after 9/11 when all brown people carry the weight of being a terrorist first and human second, could have been Middle Eastern. He had a carefully manicured thick black moustache, a slight white scar above his right eyebrow, and he appeared to gaze at something far away that no one else saw.

As the train pulled away from the platform, he removed his cap and faced all of us other riders in the car, launching into a well-rehearsed and heart-rending speech about how he'd recently lost his job and could no longer afford to feed and house his wife and children. This was a speech getting all too familiar since the days of trickle-down economics, a phrase coined decades ago during the Reagan presidency to describe rich politicians and CEO's pissing on us from somewhere over our heads. The speechmaker swore he wasn't a drug addict or bum, but that he was desperate. With an apology, he unzipped the knapsack and reached inside.

The entire car let out a collective sigh of anxiety. In these days when someone claims to be distraught and filled with despair, and then reaches into a knapsack, everyone expects a gun to come out or a bomb to go off. This time, the man was only clearing a spot for people to drop in spare change.

Once we realized he intended no harm, no one responded, including me. The sad part of this whole encounter was the realization of how cynical and self-centered we've become in the U.S. People stared at their hands, the floor, the walls, or pretended to be asleep. One man yelled, "Get out of our country." I felt like I should have given him some money but couldn't bring myself to do it because I couldn't get past my own doubts about the pan-handler's situation or his motives. Did he really have a family in need or was he simply using the story as a con? I'll never know, but I'll always wonder.

Forty years ago, I would have probably emptied my pockets. But things have changed. We live in a society where even our moral and religious leaders lie constantly and about almost everything as part of doing routine business, and this leaves me as jaded as the next person when it comes to charity. It isn't that those who choose careers of service to others have suddenly become imperfect. There have always been perverted ministers in every aspect of our society. Some preachers and priests will be perverted. Some politicians will be corrupt. Some business leaders will operate outside the law. However, in the 21st century the problem infects the system as well as some individuals within it. Now, *most* politicians will end up corrupting their office. Large numbers of preachers will succumb to greed or temptations of the flesh. CEO's run huge, multi-national corporations as if they were mafia dons. Democracy has been replaced with a self-serving capitalism on steroids.

How do we turn this lack of empathy around? Maybe a step in the right direction is to start demanding accountability from our leaders and force them to set better examples. What better time than right now when some of those leaders are fomenting rebellion and fascism? Maybe part of the answer lies in examining our own priorities as a society and focusing more on altruism than self-indulgence. Ultimately, what will be required is individual consciousness-raising. But that makes the process of becoming better collective citizens exponentially more difficult because it requires that each one of us consider on occasion what's best for the rest of us.

13. *Scenery*

As children, we often see the world literally and believe what our parents tell us the same way. Leaving my home in Princeton, Indiana, travelling south toward Evansville along State Highway 41 in the late 1950's and through the 1960's a cornucopia of strange sights unfurled along both sides of the asphalt. Rows and rows of stalks spread out like an endless sea, the depth of which grew from shallow buds to giant waves of green and then a wilted brown between Easter and Halloween. From the middle of this sea, an island of concrete block buildings surrounded a giant silo painted with the letters "Princeton Farms." When I asked my father what grew there his answer was always the same, popcorn. No matter how hard I tried, I was never able to envision the tasty salted and buttered white kernels my mother fed me by the bowlfuls at home popping out of those stalks as we watched *Gunsmoke* and *The Twilight Zone* and *Lawrence Welk* on our new black and white Motorola TV.

A few miles further as the Desoto approached the tiny village of Fort Branch a giant plaster hog rested in the front lawn of a sturdy brick home. The closer we drove to the bright white monster, the more the acrid stench that filled the air around it became. A cross between decayed earth and manure, the methane gas produced by the hog farm was a common odor in the rural areas of Southern Indiana, but beyond my sphere of knowledge at the age of ten. Whenever we passed by, I held my nose and sputtered. "What is that awful stink?" Dad never wavered in his reply. "That's the smell of money, son." I spent a lot of time sniffing quarters and dimes, even a few wrinkled dollar bills. The smell of ink and metal—yes—but never hog shit graced my olfactory senses.

Over the years many strange things came and went, notably a Barbeque Restaurant that featured lunchtime strippers, a tortilla factory, an oval dirt track for NASCAR wannabe's, a concrete block building called Lamey's Grove that housed hundreds of drunken teenagers once a week, a herd of buffalo, a racehorse training farm, and a family diner with a mechanical orchestra. Of all these sights, however, none terrified me more than a bizarre ceramic business that covered a patch of land with the most hideous lawn ornaments imaginable. Driving past the place as a small child prepared me for a bad acid trip I took in my early twenties.

These eyesores along scenic country highways were not unusual in rural Americana. It was almost as if by proximity to natural beauty, the glazed nightmares were expected to blossom as well. A rainbow of painted colors adorned the statues and birdbaths. To add to the grotesqueness of the sight of three wise men, I might have found a red baby Jesus or a green Santa Claus. Birds, fish, squirrels, gargoyles, wolves, Greek columns, and Civil War soldiers stood at attention, while mermaids and best of all pink Flamingoes lined up in rows liked cenotaphs to mark the graves of unknown departed *Phoenicopterus* fowl. And, it might have well as been a graveyard because when I drove by thirty years later most of those same ceramic items still rested in perpetuity regardless of what lay beneath them.

14. *Mamas, Don't Let Your Babies Grow Up to be Cowboys*

Mamas don't let your babies grow up to be cowboys." This is a line from a famous country and western song by Waylon Jennings. It's pretty good career advice for a lot of reasons, some of which I will mention shortly. But the mythology of the Old West is the only mythology that is truly American, which makes it important if we are to understand how we got where we are as a nation, for better or worse. Like all myths, ours is chock full of prejudice, lies, and factual inaccuracies. I'll admit that up front before the whining about how myths are chock full of prejudice, lies, and factual inaccuracies starts. Any student of human nature recognizes the duality of the human condition—the existence of love and hate, peace and violence, kindness and selfishness, logic and illogic, the ability to seek truth and at the same time lie even to ourselves—that thrives inside each individual. Those that create myths are no different than those of us who are entertained, maybe even educated, by them.

In America's heyday immediately following World War II, a new media called TV brought us Roy Rogers, Hop-a-long Cassidy, The Lone Ranger, Gene Autry, Texas John Slaughter, Cisco Kid, Matt Dillon, Paladin, Tom Mix, The Rifleman, and a dozen or so different characters played by John Wayne and Ward Bond and Ben Johnson. This list could probably continue, even be extended, to include more cowboys for the length of the page and added with a few dogs like Rin Tin Tin, Lassie, and Old Yeller. What do they all have in common? They were my boyhood heroes when television was first introduced into every home during the nineteen-fifties, and archetypal representations of the attitudes and actions that made American males great.

I'm not going to try and make a politically correct case for these TV and movie characters today, some based on real men and some fictitious. They were all white and they all fought the Injuns. The leitmotif that ran through these early TV cowboy shows was strongly influenced by racism, misogyny, a false concept of patriotism, and cultural appropriation. I'm going to acknowledge that their characters reflected the negative nationwide ideas of the white majority at that time as most literary or film characters would from history's perspective and then try to get to the positive aspects of their heroics that are worth considering in our 21st century age of moral relativity. In other words, I'm not going to throw away penicillin because it comes from mold. I'm going to use the qualities that make me healthier and try to learn what I can as I discard the poison.

Most importantly, these mythological characters exhibited some inalienable and inherent moral standards of right and wrong in common. I'm not talking about strict religious standards, but rather human ones that even religious fanatics recognize exist outside doctrinal boundaries. The Apostle Paul says, "Indeed, when Gentiles, who do not have the [Mosaic] law, do by nature things required by the law, they are a law for themselves, even though they do not have the law..." (Romans 2:14).

My childhood heroes were these men, the ones who did by nature the good things required of them for the collective betterment of the world around them, at least in stories if not in reality. They all exhibited a conscience on screen, which is what Paul is referring to. Questions such as how my decisions affect other people, what is valuable beyond the material, are we really free without accountability, among others were asked and answered in the actions these story-book heroes took. They were answered symbolically in the superhuman activities against metaphorical evil undertaken successfully, and in the ability to survive dilemmas ordinary people could not withstand.

Consider the code of one of the most successful legends in media history, The Lone Ranger, published in an article by National Public Radio on justice outside the law.

I believe...

That to have a friend, a man must be one.

That all men are created equal and that everyone has within himself the power to make this a better world.

That God put the firewood there, but that every man must gather and light it himself.

In being prepared physically, mentally, and morally to fight when for what is right.

That a man should make the most of what equipment he has.

That 'this government of the people, by the people, and for the people' shall live always

That men should live by the rule of what is best for the greatest number.

That sooner or later...somewhere...somehow...we must settle with the world and make payment for what we have taken.

That all things change but truth, and that truth alone, lives on forever.

In my Creator, my country, my fellow man.

Even though a fictitious mythology, there are some principles included in this value system that, when applied, could make the world a better place for everyone.

Clayton Moore and Jay Silverheels, actors who played The Lone Ranger and Tonto in the original series, believed it was up to them to set a good example as role models around their young fans by attempting to follow these rules. Closer scrutiny of the plots involved and dramatic outcomes for most of the early celluloid cowboys will show that these concepts were generally accepted as part of the heroic code and defined what was meant by the term "a good man." Yes, they had faults as characters and as actors representing those characters, but I will not fault them for trying to be *better* than most of society, particularly white society, at the time.

For most of my early life cowboys controlled the corral of American social mores. I was required to be polite around my elders, treat all women as *ladies*, defend the helpless, fight injustice, share with others, and be willing to serve in areas of greatest need. Those ideals were a prime motivator when I enlisted in the Marine Corps and went to Vietnam, and Vietnam, for me, was where the value system that had served me well as a young man began to fall apart.

It did for many of my friends as well. The reality of an unjust war and the finality of three million dead Americans and Vietnamese brought to light a moral relativity that had existed for centuries in the shadows and behind closed doors. Because we called Vietnam "Injun" country and ourselves cowboys did not make us right and the Vietnamese people wrong. Behind the cowboy mythology of my youth was an insidious agenda controlled by people who profit from making illusions seem real. The illusory code I chose to believe in and live by was not the real code that generated our actions.

My country had become increasingly under control by a military-industrial complex of corporations that existed for one reason, to make a profit. These entities were and are amoral. The concepts of right and wrong do not exist within their mission statements. The cowboy code in films, on TV, and in books morphed into a value system through which expediency began to dominate, the boundaries between right and wrong blurred, and the characters themselves in an attempt to appear more human based their decisions on circumstance rather than principles. The anti-hero became our hero This all means the great motivator of self-sacrifice becomes greatly diminished.

It was inevitable in the post-sixties, postmodern era for this to happen and I'm not advocating that we return to a time in our history when what seemed utopian for white middle class males was, in all honesty, a dystopian period for ethnic minorities, women, the LGBT community, and the poor. I'm simply trying to point out that our cowboy heroes had some positive things to share with us and we have, as a society, forgotten what they were. We are on the verge of constant war, overwhelming poverty, a return to virulent racism, and the destruction of education. We have already made a democratic system of elections nothing more than silent auctions of power with corporations able to elect one corrupt politician after another. In fact, this debased election process led to a vile creature with orange skin, who by his own words and actions exemplifies most of our problems, winning the highest elected office in the land. It might be in our best interest to not only learn from the negative lessons from the Old West, which is a celluloid illusion anyway, but look more closely at some of the positive ones involved in the only true American mythology from so many years ago.

I believe there is a place for moral relativity, that it is far more conducive to freedom than absolute dictated structure in life. Human actions seem most often and best served based on individual circumstance rather than categorical application of rules regardless of circumstance. But that only works when applied through the filter of a conscience, something many of my boyhood heroes exhibited even in a fictitious setting, and a concept that is continually disappearing from our social mores.

15. *For What It's Worth*

There are literally thousands of verbal snapshots with which a writer could share images of what makes America, for better or worse, the amazing place it happens to be. I'm too old to even try, so I'll leave you with a parable for your own thoughts. Maybe you've heard it before. I first heard it in from a Chinese waiter in a restaurant in some alley off Mott Street. Manhattan had a vibrant Chinatown neighborhood fifty years ago. Probably, still does. It may have originated in a time before time with Siddhartha Gautama, a guy we just call "The Buddha" now. That's the thing about parables. A good one seems to have human societies evolve around it, almost like a prophecy. Unfortunately, so do bad ones. Maybe a parable is more of a mirror than a story.

Anyway, there is a tale from ancient times about six blind men ordered to examine an elephant and report their findings. One by one they approach the beast and proceed to lay on hands. The first blind man touched the elephant's flank and said, "I have found a wall." Following him closely, the second reached and grasp the elephant's trunk. "I have found a snake," he exclaimed. At the back, a third man grabbed the tail. "I have found a rope." The fourth man, standing next to the first, grabbed the elephant's ear. "No, no," he said. "This is a huge fan." Next to last and not able to see where he was going, one of the men bumped into the elephant's thick leg. "You're all wrong. It's an old tree." Finally, the last blind man poked the tusk. "Watch out. We've found a sharp spear."

Each report was true for each of the blind men. They all had a clear image of what they had touched. Yet, each report was also false because their images were based on a *limited* perspective. If each man had been humble enough to consider that his conjectures could never be more than part of something and willing enough to work with the others, then they would have realized the whole.

www.ingramcontent.com/pod-product-compliance
Lightning Source LLC
LaVergne TN
LVHW091046150826
845673LV00002B/479

9789363540927